From the End Zone to a Wheelchair

How I Met God

Doug Smooth Harrington

Strategic Book Publishing and Rights Co.

Strategic Book Publishing and Rights Co., LLC
USA | Singapore

www.sbpra.net

For information about special discounts for bulk purchases, please
contact Strategic Book Publishing and Rights Co. Special Sales, at
bookorder@sbpra.net.

ISBN: 978-1-68235-621-0

Artwork and front cover designed created by Gary McKelvey

Book Design: Suzanne Kelly

DEDICATIONS

I dedicate this book to my children and grandchildren: my beautiful daughter Da'Quoiya Janae, my handsome son Roderick Tyrone, and my sweet grandchildren Jaiden Lee and Jordyn Rhene. I thank you all for your love and support musically and upon completing this book.

I want you all to know some of the things that occurred to me in my life. I had to overcome some things in my life and I don't want you to make some of the mistakes and bad choices that I made. Now you may read some things that may make you uncomfortable. Some things will jar your memory, and other things you may have no clue as to what I'm talking about. I have been through a lot and I'm happy and proud to be your father and grandfather! I also want to thank my mom Evelyn Harrington for never giving up on me!

This book is also dedicated in memory of my father, George Harrington, and my brother, Jeffrey Harrington, who both are no longer here with us but their spirit lives within me. I also want to thank my sisters, Joyce and Donna, and my sister-in-law, Larissa, for their love and support and guidance and all my uncles, aunties, cousins, nieces, and nephews.

I love y'all!
In Jesus Name, Amen!

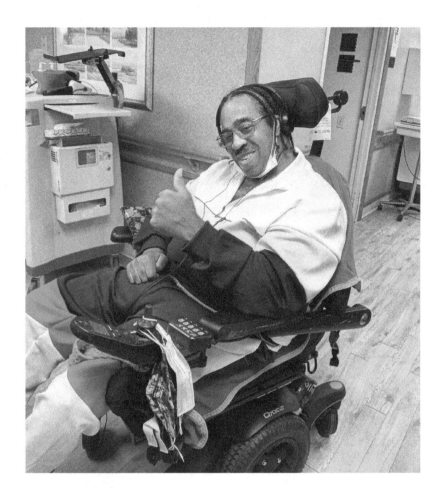

To my mom,
I just wanted to thank you for your love and support
through the good and the bad years of my life,
and while we both were still breathing.
My queen!
I love you

ENDORSEMENTS

Eugene Head—

I am a retired teacher, coach, dean of students, elementary school principal, and middle school principal with forty years of experience in the field of education. This book is a quick and easy read that is very insightful. It is written in a style that allows you to envision the text like a movie picture in your mind. The book gives an insider's view into a life and world that few people knew existed and had little or no knowledge of. It shows us that you cannot always believe what your eyes are seeing. Sometimes the grass is not greener on the other side. We see that God is always present in our lives even when we don't know it and are not looking for Him. The many trials and tribulations that Doug experienced are truly fascinating. The journey that Doug took toward the "light" is nothing short of amazing and is outlined in a wonderful manner. This book is a must read.

Dr. Vernice "Trala" Wright, NCC, LCPC, CADC, CODP-I, CAMS-II—

I was so amazed by this book and the journey of my dear friend, Doug Harrington. This autobiography of his life is a true testimony of struggle, survival, strength, and success! He showed how a victim can be victorious through the Lord. I am a licensed clinical professional therapist and a doctorate of advanced counseling-psychology, aka Counseling Education and Supervision (C.E.S). I have worked in the field of mental health and substance abuse since 1999 and opened a Prit Avenue practice here in my hometown (Waukegan) to guide people with a journey and struggles similar to Doug. His story is a true testimony of strength, hope, faith, and courage! Therapists often question if it's nature or nurture that impacts one's life! Doug's book took us on a journey of how both, nature and nurture, created the blueprint of who we are, were, and can be! Thank you, Mr. Doug Harrington, for sharing your life, faith, and journey with the world! It's an easy read that allows anyone who reads it to visualize your true life experience and believe that change is possible! I feel honored to be included in the acknowledgement of a profoundly honest manuscript written to help and encourage others. Thank you, my dear friend Doug! The Lord has truly carried you through this journey. I'm honored to know you! This is a true "must read."

Cara Riggs, Principal, Teacher, and Author of *Hope in the Urban Schools: Love Stories—*

From the End Zone to a Wheelchair: How I Met God *by Doug Smooth Harrington is truly a work of inspiration. Doug's journey through life, challenges, and health issues makes one's own problems seem miniscule. Through faith, perseverance, and determination, Doug has battled like a soldier to forge on no matter what. Be ready to be amazed and awed at how his life's lessons continue to show others that God's grace manifests in all we do when we continue to believe. A quick but powerful read, indeed.*

Illinois State Representative Rita Mayfield—

This book is refreshingly honest and goes deep into Doug's soul and emerges with a confession that will bring tears to your eyes. From the first page to the last, you will be taken on a roller coaster ride of sex, overindulgence, and self-hate. Doug's journey to God didn't start with his accident; it started years before in college when his battle with demons first began. Journey down the down the rabbit hole with Doug and reach for the light. This book is inspirational.

Amon Rashidi—

I am a father, artist, activist, and subject matter expert in the field of youth violence and capacity as a consultant to YouthBuild USA. I was a guest speaker in Waukegan where Doug was working as a life skills teacher at Youth Conservation Corporation (YCC). During my stay I had an opportunity to visit their studio and meet his brother Jeff and a few other family members. I reference this because according to the book, he was still fighting his addiction demons during that time. This book gives you a glimpse of how those demons came about. Doug takes you on a journey through his childhood traumas and how his traumas unleashed desires that were detrimental to his life. I am honored that he asked me to contribute to this book, because it is a shared reflection of his life. Doug's characterization of the times he grew up in took me on a journey down memory lane. Once I began reading I didn't want to stop. His writing style gives you a visual interpretation of each scenario that he shares. I laughed, I grimaced, I related in some instances, and I was saddened in others. It's full of twists and turns and just when you think he's got it together, well, I'll let you be the judge.

Lamont Taylor, CADC, CODP, MAATP—

As a local pastor, activist, and parent of five, I strongly recommend that everyone who has ever experienced adversity and heartache to read this book. Douglas has gone down deep into his soul and found the right combination of words to read, again and again. If you're looking for a true, authentic, and heartfelt pick-me-up, this is the book.

INTRODUCTION

This book was written to provide inspiration to anyone who may be suffering from some form of addiction, and for those who may be on the fence when it comes to believing in God. You are not alone. This book will also reveal to people some things without saying any names of the individuals and/ or participants, let alone the different types of addiction I was suffering from. The challenge to me writing this book was not throwing anyone under the bus, all while remaining true to God! So if you are looking for a book with quotes and scripture throughout, then you have selected the wrong book! I know my haters are gonna read this book to find out what they can about me. I don't really care! If God is for me, then who can be against me! I would like to share with you my life experiences through trial and triumph, ups and downs, as I fight through the battle of addiction.

The God I serve has blessed me and shown me grace and mercy throughout my life. Unfortunately, I was too hardheaded to be aware of it! There are some of you that can relate to my struggles because you have been through it in your past. Your individual stories and years of sobriety have given me the hope and strength that I need to succeed in my fight with addiction. You know who you are. Some folks were able to stop cold turkey. Others got help from a drug rehabilitation center. Some were forced by their commitment to the state. But what about the ones who wanted to stop cold turkey but couldn't? What about the ones who went to a rehabilitation center or a jail cell only to get out and resume the same lifestyle? What about those people you would never suspect were addicted, or battling through addiction, because of the way they carried themselves?

You just never knew or suspected that particular person was using drugs or still is abusing drugs.

I have met numerous individuals from all walks of life, functioning like normal human beings for years. Yet, they were using drugs for whatever reason they chose to use them. It starts out as being fun and often used as entertainment for one's enjoyment. Then it becomes needed by the body to perform everyday functions. Some of you will realize that I'm either talking about us or you can relate to the situation because you were there or something similar happened to you.

I need y'all to understand that none of what you are about to read is a lie! Everything that occurred happened. I even reached out to several friends and teammates and asked them if they had a story they wanted to share in this book. Now I'm not bragging, boasting, or trying to make myself look good, as you try to figure out who I'm talking to or about or if it is you. I'm not trying to create any new enemies. I've got enough jealous and envious haters already. Remember that no one knows I'm talking about you but me! And I will never mention any names. So you are protected! With that being said, it's time to tell my story.

TABLE OF CONTENTS

CHAPTER 1
1866 North Maud

I can still remember it as if it was yesterday, crossing the street and walking through the alley leaving 1866 North Maud. No one but me and my grandma headed to the store to buy some breakfast food. I was going because I knew that if I went, my grandma was gonna buy me some candy! So we proceeded to walk in the alleyway in the inner city of Chicago, Illinois, Northside. A walk that we had made plenty of times before, only this time it would be different.

The alley was a long stretch of paved blacktop, lined with garbage cans and a smell that I just can't describe. The garbage cans were in the rear of the two-story homes looking like they were connected to one another. The alleyway was the back of residences and local businesses. It ran directly into another alley with street openings located at each end. We were entering the section of the alley in which there was nothing but building after building—no homes. As we were walking down this alley, I noticed two shady-looking characters approaching in the direction in which we walked towards the alley's end. It was then one of the men pulled out a knife and approached my grandma demanding that she give him her purse!

Now I was ready to fight but I was very small in size and age and would be no match for the masked men. My grandma looked over at me and reached into her purse as she pleaded to our attackers by saying, "Please don't hurt my grandson. He's just a baby!" On the other hand, I was ready to fight and ready to protect my grandma at all costs, but this was serious! I know I had heard of the stick-up kid. And thought what I would do, but this was the real deal. So she gave our assailants all the cash she

1

had and some food stamps. I noticed she didn't give them any of her change and my grandma was known for having change (she kept her some change, y'all). The robbers grabbed the money and food stamps and ran out of the alley. I wanted to chase after them so bad but I knew I was just too little. If I caught up to them what was I gonna do? And my grandma was just too old to do anything.

She asked me if I was okay as we proceeded to walk back towards the house. The same alleyway, a route we were so used to taking, seemed so much longer now as we headed back home. Once we got inside I was called to her bedroom and she told me not to mention this incident to anyone, including my mom and "especially not your uncles!"

Now, my mom was one of two girls in the family. She was really referring to my twelve uncles. That's right, I said twelve, twelve uncles—young men I knew and wanted to be like. I didn't understand why I was told not to tell them, but I had an idea why. She made me promise not to tell them, so I haven't told anyone for all these years.

I was raised in a big family. I had one older brother and two older sisters, plus my mom and dad. This was my family. My dad's family consists of him, my uncle, and my aunt, alongside my grandparents. My mom's family, on the other hand, was huge! There were only two girls, my mom and my aunt, but there were twelve boys. My uncles were better known as the Thomas Brothers. Each and every last one of them could play a musical instrument, a reflection of my grandad, who could play everything. And I do mean everything! So it was common to see musical instruments just laying around in the basement as we played as children.

It seemed like every member of my family knew how to play something, so I always felt that I had to learn to play something to be accepted by my family. Although this was not true, at the time I didn't know any better. So I was enticed by the drums. My uncle would show me some things and I would jump on the drums every chance that I got. I remember that they would take a smoke break and go outside in the backyard, then I would jump on the drums. As I grew older I became curious about the guitar, a six-stringed instrument that my brother was intrigued by. My brother was six years older than me, but I was very observant for my age. I watched my uncles as they gave him some tips about playing the guitar. My uncles were jamming. The band featured a brass section that consisted of a saxophone, a trumpet, and a trombone. They were bad too! That's bad meaning good! It was normal for them to have several women at their rehearsals. And I was watching everything and everybody. There were so many other women around that my aunts began to sing background on certain songs. I think they did it to keep an eye on my uncles. They had a name I thought was sending a message to the band's groupies. They called themselves the Main Squeeze.

Meanwhile, my brother moved from the guitar to the piano. I was confused and didn't understand why he was trying that new instrument; it just seemed so much harder to play. My brother, however, still played guitar and even convinced one of my uncles to give him his very own. I was jealous and got mad because I wanted my own. He would take the guitar home with him and practice everything my uncles had shown him. He would master what they showed him and then he would teach me. My dad saw this too—he plays the bass guitar. It looks just like a guitar only the bass guitar has four thicker strings and a much deeper sound. The more my dad would teach my brother, the more I would watch, just waiting for my opportunity to play.

We would continue to emulate my uncles as we grew older, dreaming that one day I would be good enough to play with them. I recall one day my uncle and I were to go to the store for my grandma and get a few items for dinner, so we went across the street, taking the shortcut through the alleyway to the store. This time we encountered two males who jumped from behind the garbage containers in the alley. They wanted whatever money we had, but my uncle wasn't having it! A fight ensued. I was punching and kicking and before you knew it, our would-be robbers took off running past the garbage cans from where they came.

3

We then proceeded to the store to get the items that my grandma was waiting for. I got my candy and the items my grandma was cooking for dinner that night. In the meantime, I was busy bragging to my cousin about the fight and the danger we had just escaped. I didn't know I was talking so loud because my grandma heard me and asked me and my uncle what happened. We both explained to her what happened, and she told my granddad and my parents. Not long after that we moved to Waukegan.

CHAPTER 2

Waukegan

Waukegan is a suburb located about forty-five minutes north of the Chicago area. We moved to St. James Street, located on the city's south side. Unfortunately, I have a very bad memory of us living on that street—that memory being the death of our dog, Coffee. Coffee was a great dog, mixture of collie and Labrador. She was a tan fireball and very smart for a dog. My aunt from Chicago had given her to us. She was a great dog, and I messed up—that's the only way you can say it. Let me tell you what happened.

See, we had just returned from a Lake Michigan beach in downtown Waukegan. We pulled up to our home entering the driveway. We were all exiting the vehicle, except for my dad. I was in the backseat on the driver side. My mom was in the front passenger seat with one of my sisters in the middle, and my brother was sitting in the rear passenger seat with my other sister in the middle and Coffee. Everybody proceeded to get out the right side of my dad's clean Buick LeSabre.

Now, my dad had many cars to choose from. He worked at Johnson Motors at the time, a local factory located on the lakefront that made fishing boat motors. My mom was working at Abbott's Laboratory. It was a company that made all kinds of different medicine and medical devices. They both had really good jobs and made really good money, so my family and I had nice things.

As we got out of the car, I didn't see that the dog had exited on the right side with my brother and sister. I was on the left side and I began to call her name. The dog proceeded to come to me because I had called her, while my father was backing out of the driveway. Coffee was safe until I had called her name. She quickly went from being out of harm's way into being in harm's way! Then my dad, not knowing what was going on, proceeded to drive out of the driveway. He had accidentally run over the dog.

Coffee laid in the driveway motionless. We all went to her aid but there was nothing that any of us could do. She was just lying there in the driveway and my entire family was in tears. My sisters were devastated. They were in real agony over the dog's death. I knew deep down inside that it was my fault! I shouldn't have ever called her name. I have to live with that guilt for the rest of my life. I don't think or ever recall us owning another dog after this accident.

After a few years at this location, my parents found an even bigger and better home. We then moved to 928 North Jackson Street on the west side of Waukegan. It was at this address my life as a kid was about to change.

Now I refuse to give the details, location, or any information that would expose individuals who dramatically changed my life. I said that I would not say any names or anything. The last thing I need is to lead a trail to somebody and get them blamed or thrown under the bus. I was sexually assaulted by a family member! No, not a member of my immediate family. Let me make sure I make that clear. I was assaulted, led, coached, and seduced into sexual acts. These acts were performed on me, and I was still in elementary school! I was told not to tell anyone, so I didn't. However, it felt really good to me! I remember I didn't have any hair on my genitals, nothing. But I was packing for my age. That meant my penis was a good size. I was told that I was larger than most guys and bigger than some guys who were older than me. At the time, I really didn't understand what was going on.

I remember the very first time like it was yesterday. I was told to sit in a chair naked, so I took off my shirt then took off my pants and underwear. I think they were some Spider-Man underwear too, I'm not sure! Anyway, I sat down and looked around the room. The next thing I knew she was putting her mouth all over my penis for a few minutes. I remember it kinda tickled me but it felt good! Then she sat down on top of me, and proceeded to go up and down as if we were on a seesaw. This went on for several minutes. When she was done she made it very clear to me not to tell anybody. It was our little secret. So I agreed not to tell anyone because I was afraid, thinking that I had pissed inside her. Now, I didn't know anything about sex or ejaculation. I just knew I had pissed inside her and if I told I was gonna be in big trouble!

This act went on for several months. She would do this to me every chance she got, and I enjoyed it every time. It got to the point where she started bragging and bringing her girlfriends along. They would take turns putting their mouth on me before sitting on me. Now, not knowing anything about sex, I was enjoying the feeling that I was feeling. It was something that I couldn't explain.

This went on for several more months. Then I noticed a wet stain in my underwear. Then it started to hurt when I would use the bathroom. I didn't know what was going on. I didn't know what to do, so I told my mom that it hurt when I urinated. She informed my dad and they both sat me down to find out what was happening to me and why I was feeling this way. They began to question me, but I didn't reveal any information. I knew if I told them it would create a lot of problems, so I kept my mouth shut and me and my dad ended up going to the Lake County Clinic to get this situation fixed. There was no talk about the birds and the bees. It was too late at that point, but he did end up explaining sex to me.

When we arrived at the clinic, I got a shot in my behind. After the doctor started asking me all these questions, my dad began to get defensive. Then the nurse started to ask me all types of questions. If you were wondering, Child Protective Services were notified but they were not as responsive as they are in today's world. I also received some Jimmy hats from the clinic. Those are better known as condoms. I was shown how to use them and put them on and everything. Remember, I was still in elementary school. I was forced to grow up quickly. My parents

7

had no clue as to what was happening to me, and I wasn't telling them! I remember they tried to figure it out, but they couldn't. They didn't know when or where. They kept trying to figure it out. They even put me on "lockdown," as I call it, and forbade me to go anywhere, but this only lasted for so long. Eventually, they would loosen my rope. What I was experiencing felt really good to me, plus I was told to keep it a secret. I wasn't gonna tell a soul! My mom was still skeptical of the situation, however, so she was still searching and investigating, trying to get to the truth.

It was then I was really introduced to sports by my mom and my brother. I recall staying up late watching Dr. J in basketball games and Walter Payton highlights during football season. Just watching these two, I knew I wanted to be like them and became very consumed with sports.

CHAPTER 3
A Young Star in the Making

We were young, just trying to have fun. We played every sport you could think of{. All of my friends at the time played on a team or some organized league. See, we didn't have cell phones or social media, the internet, PlayStations, or Xboxes back then. It was a normal to ride by Glen Flora School on Jackson Street and see a group of kids outside playing sports during bad weather. I recall shoveling the basketball court or the batter's box for us to play baseball, where we played strike out regularly. We used to love playing football in the snow. We would pretend to be the Chicago Bears. Every one of us loved tackling each other and sliding in the snow. At halftime, we would go to someone's house and warm up and drink some hot chocolate. Then we would go back out and continue playing ball.

Sometimes, we would play pon pon tackle—a game where one person would start out in the middle of a field, tackling as many people as they could as they ran by. Once you got tackled you had to tackle somebody else. This game continued until there was nobody left to tackle. I was usually the last person left to be to be tackled. They had a lot of different names for this game we played. A lot of people called it Smear the Queer or Kill 'Em. We never really paid any attention to the time. Nobody really owned a watch or had a watch on, so when the street lights came on, the game was over. Whoever was leading at the time the lights came on won! When the game was over, everybody would then pick up their equipment, pack it up, and head for the crib. That's home for some of y'all!

We played football, basketball, and baseball during their seasons, and we played those sports when they weren't in season—with no regards to the weather. We didn't care how cold or hot it was, or if it was raining. I was still very young but I began to excel and separate myself from my age group, as far as skills were concerned. I'm not bragging or boasting, but you can ask any of the guys that were there and they will tell you, I was clearly a little bit better than my peers at each sport. Baseball was my most successful sport, although I didn't know it. I played in the outfield and first base. The second baseman and I were the only two brothers on our team. Sometimes, we were the only two brothers on the field, but every time we played we showed out. I was selected to the all-star team every year. They had a regular all-star team and a traveling all-star team, and I was selected for both! This wasn't normal.

I also recall going to Wrigley Field on the regular with my grandma to see the Cubs. I wanted to be like this Cub outfielder named José Cardenal, who was really good, had a lot of hair under his baseball cap, and played in the outfield. As I grew

older my grandma would let me go to the games by myself. I would just hop on the L train, located down the street from the house. A ride to Wrigley Field was a straight shot from my grandma's house. One of my uncles would also take me to Comiskey Park, the home of the Chicago White Sox. They had an outfielder named Oscar Gamble, who was also really good and had a lot of hair underneath his baseball cap too.

As I continued to get better, we started playing baseball and basketball games in different areas of the city. A friend of mine had a regulation half of a basketball court in his backyard. It was there I began to make a name for myself. I was good and getting better. I was still too young to play organized football, my favorite. So I then begged and pleaded and eventually convinced my aunt to falsify my age on my birth certificate so that I could participate in a football league.

I had an appetite for sports. I was playing at every opportunity no matter who was playing. I used to love playing basketball against those who were bigger and older than I was. It was at these games I began to show out. I would play with my uncle all

11

the time too. I did have my nemeses and stiff competition. Don't get it twisted. I was playing against some of the best competition on a daily basis. We played in this tournament at Bedrosian Park, located on the south side of the city. It was equivalent to the great Rucker Park in Brooklyn, New York. Now, these guys in the tournament could ball too! We didn't win, but playing against bigger and stronger competition caused me to elevate my game, remain on top, and be the first player selected when we were picking during pickup games regularly, regardless of what sport we were playing at that time. I had a sidekick too who was as good as me, if not better, at certain sports. He didn't play baseball, but he loved football and basketball. I think we were playing with the Bombsquad, a team with the best middle school players in the city. This team was created a few years prior because the lack of funding eliminated basketball as a team sport at the middle school level. Now, my older friends began to call me Artist, in reference to Artis Gilmore, a left-handed big man who played for the Chicago Bulls. I was left-handed and a big man amongst my peers. My partners didn't like the name.

I'm not sure if my baseball buddies or basketball buddies gave me the nickname Smooth. They said it was because I did all things: I played football, basketball, baseball; I was fast; I played the drums, guitar, and piano; and I used to be a disc jockey. I did all these things and did them well. All gifts from God; however, I didn't know any better. My peers began to say, "Ole boy pretty Smooth with his game," and the nickname just stuck.

My mom said my dad had a different name for me way back then. I was really young and don't remember, but he called me Midget—short for Midget Man. He was amazed at all the things I could do at such a young age! Even though I had a hunger for sports, I still enjoyed having sex with girls. I began to venture out and convince different girls, some older, some younger, to have sex with me. It was pretty easy. Most of the girls were curious and eager to have sex back then. They were eager to lose their virginity. It didn't hurt that I looked handsome and had a long Jheri curl, the style at that time.

CHAPTER 4

Growing Pains

A t this point I didn't know Jesus from God! I didn't attend church like some people. My granddad wasn't a believer of the church at the time, so it's fair to say that he wasn't a big church fan. This attitude rubbed off on my uncles, which eventually rubbed off on me.

Now my mom, on the other hand, began to attend church on the regular. You could see her attending the Shiloh Baptist Church. This church was located directly across the street from the YMCA where we would sometimes play basketball. My mom became actively involved in the church, yet she didn't push her religion on any of the family, which allowed us to come to know Jesus later on in life. At this point on the weekends, I would spend the night at one of my friends' houses or host a few friends at my crib. I can remember we were running from the living room to the dining room playing Nerf hoop in my house. I also recall I was with a bunch of my football teammates at my friend's house when I had my first experience using drugs. I remember we were all in the basement, talking about practice, certain plays, girls, and stuff. We were also watching TV and playing pool and now talking exclusively about girls. You know, the normal things that teenage boys would talk about.

It was then my friend reached underneath their Curtis Mathes floor model television and grabbed a shoe case box top. It was full of weed! He recently had found his father's stash, and he wanted to show it off to us. We were all curious about how the weed would affect us. So we rolled up a couple of joints. We all had seen this process before, so rolling up a joint was no big deal. After the weed was rolled up and the sticky part of the rolling paper was licked, we started smoking and coughing. None of us really knew what we were doing. Everyone was acting as if they had smoked weed before, but I knew deep down this was everyone's first time smoking weed. I'm wondering if y'all remember the commercial with the eggs and the frying pan? And the announcer said, "This is your brain. This is your brain on drugs. Any questions?" Well, it was nothing like the commercial (ha-ha).

Once we stopped smoking, I remember we started laughing! I mean, we were laughing at everything. Things that weren't even funny we were laughing at. Once the laughter subdued, I realized that I was hungry as hell, and I wasn't the only one! So we then raided the kitchen and it seemed like we were eating up everything on site. We didn't realize at the time that we all had the munchies.

There was another incident that I recall. I was spending the night at what I considered my home away from home. It was there that I left the basement to go upstairs and get my munchie on. It was normal for my mother from another brother to make a cake on the weekends to prevent us from eating up everything else. To make a long story short, I accidentally spilt the milk carton. I had milk everywhere, and the cleanup was massive! Now this keeps on happening to me on a regular basis. I guess I was a little clumsy too back in the day. Once I started to spill the Kool-Aid, I heard it from my friends. On the weekends I was given the nickname "The Spiller" and was banned from gathering any liquids in the house!

CHAPTER 5
Webster

We were attending Daniel Webster Middle School. I was focused and watching the athletes in the local high schools. My brother had been playing the guitar with a group of friends called the Golden Touch Band. They would be jamming, practicing right in the living room in our house. My parents were at work so they didn't know anything until one day they had forgotten a microphone and a microphone stand right there in the living room for my mom to find. I was busy trying to duplicate whatever my brother was doing. I was a bass guitar player but I was willing to learn the lead guitar (just like my brother) so we could form our own band. So I got together with a few of my friends and we formed a band and called it Eclipse.

Some folks didn't understand how the band members were all in high school except me. I was still in middle school but I could play, plus I had leadership skills and experience from just watching my uncles and my brother's band. I hung out with an older crowd of people. I recall the first time we were in a real, professional soundproof studio. I will never forget it. Now, I could play the guitar but I was still learning. We recorded this original song called "Dance With Me" and the engineer of the studio had put some feedback and delay on my guitar solo. And we all just tripped out! All of a sudden he had me sounding like I was Jimi Hendrix or Eddie Van Halen or somebody.

There was another incident that took place that I wanted to add but I couldn't remember, so I contacted a member of our band and he shared with me his thoughts. We had opened for my brother's band, and as we began playing I realized we were playing it in the wrong key. So the band was playing this song, a song we'd played many times before, only this time it sounded strange. In the middle of our song I started calling out loud "Hold up, hold up!" though it's not clear what my exact words were. But I said something like, "Come on, fellas, that's not how we rehearsed it," then I immediately started playing the song in the right key. The drummer hit a snare roll and the bass joined in and we started jamming and finished the song strong. Now the audience began to applaud and cheer because they thought it was a part of our show, but the band members knew we'd just dodged a bullet and this little young dude saved us!

I was enjoying middle school at the time, and I wasn't sure which high school I would attend, West or East. You see, Waukegan had two high schools at the time: the Waukegan West Raiders and the Waukegan East Bulldogs. The West Campus was known for its football program, and the East Campus was popular because of its basketball program, so I would attend both schools' athletic games and watch the players from both schools in each sport. We lived in the East Campus zoning area; however, my brother and sisters all attended the West Campus. I remember studying the running backs, defensive backs, and the playmakers as they participated in high school football games. I also recall watching the guards and forwards shoot deep jump shots long before the three-point line was even drawn up on the court. This was high school basketball at its finest.

Right about this time guys were talking about their first sexual experiences, and I was busy trying to get girls to practice oral sex on a banana, then try it on me. Yes, I was mannish, freaky, whorish, whatever you want to call it. I was just trying to get mine and I didn't care who hurt in the process. Now our football team …

The Lightweight was off the chain! I have never played with a more talented group of young men. We had talent and playmakers all over the field. I felt bad for the other team. We were in the huddle discussing whose turn it was to score the

next touchdown. It was ridiculous. We went two years in a row without losing a game or being scored on. I remember when we were finally scored on in the last game of the season, my teammates and I didn't handle it very well. There was crying and bickering amongst us—something that had never occurred on this team before. It was the first time we had controversy amongst our team. We were faced with a real adverse situation. As time was running out, I lined up with our kickoff return team. Then the coach yelled out my name and said, "Harrington, we need a big play out of you!" Then the kicker placed the ball on the tee. He waited for the official to blow his whistle a signal to begin play. He kicked the ball off the tee and the wind brought it right to me. My sidekick was back there with me, and he began leading me up the field. He delivered a crushing block in which I simply cut off. A cut here and a block there and I was gone down the sidelines for an eighty-four-yard kickoff return for a touchdown! The same teammate who was crying was now

18

jumping for joy, knowing he made the key block that sprung me for a touchdown. It was a great feeling that came across me. As I went into the end zone, I watched my teammates celebrate on our sideline. We knew we had a really talented football team.

As football season came to an end, a few of the guys were selected to hoop with the Bombsquad. I think I mentioned that team before, a group of middle school basketball players selected as the best upcoming talent in the city of Waukegan. The squad had a reputation to live up to. It was those guys who played before us. They had put the smack down on their opponents so we knew we had to come on with it. Now I'm having trouble remembering some things, or is it what they call writer's block? Whatever it is, I reached out to two of my teammates and asked them what they could remember so that I could add it to my book, and this is what they gave me to share.

We were playing I believe it was Zion, and it was like maybe four seconds to halftime and we were down by one point. My homie, who's no longer with us (RIP), takes the ball out and passes it to me. I turned towards the basket and let it fly from half court and I nailed it! We were only up two going into the third quarter, but that one shot was a game changer. The momentum was on our side, and we ended up winning the game. Our opponents were broken after that; you could see it in their eyes. Now when he texted me this, I couldn't remember any of it. All I could do was say "Wow! Did I do that-t-t-t?" (in my Steve Urkel voice). I don't know how many times I went down the hill to Webster Junior High School and played basketball inside and outside against top-notch competition. This only made me a better all-around ballplayer. Even though we had success as a basketball team, the majority of us thought we had a better chance for success in a football environment, so we chose to attend Waukegan West.

Even though I was into sports big time, I still managed to find time to have sex at every chance that I got! Okay, let me try to clean this up as best that I can. Instead of saying the words *sex* and *oral sex*, I will use the terminology we used back then, and that's the words *back* (as in we're having sex from the back or doggy-style) and *helmet cleaned*, which was oral sex. Remember, my mom and my daughter are going to read this book too!

You know, it's funny because a friend of mine was asking me about this book, so I asked him if there was a memory he wanted to share. I was thinking it would be a sports-related memory. He said, "I remember every day after school you would use our basement and take so-and-so with you, be gone for about thirty minutes, then we would go to your house and watch you play the guitar like a grown-ass man. And we were both only eleven years old!" He told me this and all I could say was "Wow! Did I do that-t-t?" (in my Steve Urkel voice).

CHAPTER 6

Raiders

At Waukegan West my freshman year, we had so much talent on the football field it was ridiculous. I mean, we were three deep at the skilled positions easily. The guys that listed numbers two and three would have been starters for any other school. Unfortunately, they saw what I saw and decided to take their talents elsewhere rather than sit on the bench. They knew their potential. The majority of them went across town to our rivals, the Waukegan East Bulldogs. We were ready as freshmen at the high school. And we were treated like freshmen too!

One thing I remember very vividly was the upperclassmen wouldn't allow us freshmen into the Raider Den. The den was a separate room filled with lockers in a closed off area of the locker room itself. It had a musty aroma spewing from it. It was a place where the upperclassmen would gather to meet and get dressed, and the freshmen were not allowed—period! No matter how good you were or thought you were, if you were a freshman on the Raiders, the Raider Den was off limits.

As time went by, I became more accustomed to the school. The coaches knew who I was, but the teachers also knew who I was too. My brother and sisters all attended the school and I was the fourth Harrington to enroll. In fact, one of my sisters was a senior at the time of my enrollment. She was very popular amongst the student body. She had taken me under her wing, but she didn't know at that time I was getting some back and my helmet was cleaned by her friends! As I learned how to skip and attend certain classes, my brother had recently purchased a very expensive piece of musical equipment. It was the Yamaha

21

MT44, a four-track recording studio that was a top-of-the-line device designed to record musical creations.

Our musical prowess and creativity was evident each and every time we went downstairs in the basement to make music. This area was quickly becoming similar to the environment that we grew up in watching my uncles, the Thomas Brothers, rehearse in Chicago. My uncles all had a gift from God, but nobody acknowledged it. So how did I know that I had a gift too? My brother was accumulating musical instruments and equipment so that we could develop that gift we had and take it to another level.

My gift was from God, but I didn't realize it at the time. I was able to play all the instruments and I played by ear—to be more specific, anything that I heard on the bass guitar I could play, anything! At the same time, the baseball coach tracked me down and wanted to know why I hadn't been out on the field with my teammates. I told him I was taking the time to focus on becoming a better football and basketball player, and he believed me. But in reality, I was using that free time to conquer me some back and to get my helmet cleaned. A bad choice on my behalf because baseball was my best sport.

We had won our conference in football our freshmen year. The expectations were high coming into my sophomore year. I recall we were playing in our first game of the season. Who would have thought during the second play of the game our quarterback would break his arm? Now, we in the huddle were looking at each other all crazy because we never practiced with a second-string quarterback, so the coach calls a timeout and pulls us all to the sidelines. Then he says, "Harrington, you're gonna be our quarterback because you know all the plays!" And everybody looked at me all crazy. They knew that I couldn't pass a lick! Now I take pride in being a good football player. I just had a problem throwing the football. I mean, it even looked crazy with number twenty-three underneath the center. I don't think I completed a single pass that day.

Well, we ended up losing that game. For some reason I thought our coach would find a suitable replacement, but unfortunately that didn't happen. He told me that I was the best man for the job, so "Deal with it!" I was like "Okay."

I recall at first I was really pissed off, trying to think of any and every reason why I shouldn't be the quarterback of this football team. I realized the situation wasn't gonna change anytime soon, so I might as well make the best of it. I then began to listen to my close partners and started to study college quarterbacks that ran the wishbone offense that we run—the University of Oklahoma and the University of Minnesota, to name a few. My teammates and I began to stay after practice to work on a few things we needed to work on. By the fourth game of our season, the stands were full for the sophomore games. This was new ground. People didn't really come to see the sophomores, unless you were family and friends. We had varsity players, alumni players, freshmen players, along with family, friends, and fans, all attending our game! And we really put on a show.

I was actually a running back playing quarterback. I instinctively knew when to pitch the football and about pitching the football downfield. We played some good football, exciting the crowd with every play. I think we had as many or more people attending our games as the varsity. We won some games but not our conference title. The fans knew I still couldn't pass a lick! We ended up being a pretty good football team.

Now a lot of the guys had to make that transition from football to basketball, including me. We had a decent basketball team.

The Hoop Squad is a name that schools used to describe their basketball team, and I used it to bring attention to our basketball program. I recall that East Campus had the basketball tradition. They were known for good basketball, so I had to do something to bring attention to us. So I recorded this song in my brother's studio called "Hoop Squad" and designed these jackets that all the basketball players wore, which were green and white. Absent was the Raider gold. This was something different, and it had our nickname and number on the front, a raider on the sleeve, and a Waukegan West Raider on the back around a hand spinning a basketball on its fingertips. A lot of people didn't know that I was the one who designed these jackets.

I remember we had a game against some school, and we got dressed in two separate locker rooms. This wasn't a normal locker room. We felt like they were trying to split up our team. We felt segregated. Some of my teammates became very upset about this. After the game, my teammates begin breaking lockers and then flat out breaking into everything! I was right along with my teammates. We had stolen all their shoes and everything in those lockers. We all agreed that we wouldn't wear their shoes to school. Everybody complied except one person. He wore his shoes to practice the very next day and we all ended up in the principal's office! We were busted, and everyone had to return their shoes or be expelled from the team and school and face criminal charges. They were gonna suspend the entire team, but they didn't. I think the administration was embarrassed enough and didn't want to deal with the situation any more than they had to.

Now, there was an area in the rear of the building at Waukegan West High School that we called "Smoker Lane." This was where students would go to smoke cigarettes. But it seems like half of the students went out there to smoke pinners! A pinner was a small marijuana joint that sold for a dollar. It was common to see everyone outside before or after lunch smoking pinners. I remember one of the girls got really sick and threw up on the floor. The security guard on duty was also our janitor. He was assisting the young lady so he called me out to go to the custodial room and retrieve his mop bucket. He took the key off his key ring and extended his arm in my direction. I reached out, grabbed the key, and proceeded to get the mop bucket out of storage. This particular storage area is located down the hallway from the cafeteria, right before you enter the boys' locker room near the stairs. I got the mop bucket, returned to the cafeteria, and they were gone, so I ended up cleaning up the mess off of the floor. In the process of cleaning the floor I totally forgot about the key he gave me, and the security guy forgot too. My mom was doing laundry and found the key, along with some rolling papers, inside my pants pockets. She confronted me about it and I lied and I made some kinda excuse. I probably said they belonged to one of my teammates.

Speaking of teammates, I reached out to my favorite Hoop Squad teammate and asked him if he had a story to share, and he told me that he remembered sophomore year and we were hooping and "Duck Hunt" had just come out on Nintendo. I was playing the point guard position and during the game, I asked my teammates who got a duck trying to guard them. For those that don't know, a duck was a weak link player on the opposing team. So he responded and I did. I then smiled at him and I said "Shoot him down" as I passed him the ball almost every time, each time encouraging him to kill that duck! Well, he had over thirty points that night. He went on to tell me that I made it fun to play basketball. All I could say was "Wow! Did I do that-t-t-t?" (in my Steve Urkel voice).

CHAPTER 7
Southside

I had spent many nights on Waukegan's southside on South Avenue and 13th Street. I had true friends who stayed on these streets or a block over either way. There was the Duplex and Lyons Court. Anybody who grew up in there could tell you that it was a bunch of good people that stayed within this area. They could also tell you that this area was no joke either!

I can't remember when I started using the drug cocaine. Cocaine usage was on the rise. In fact, it was like everybody was using it. You see, cocaine or crack cocaine affects everybody differently. Cocaine is a stimulant drug, widely used for entertainment and enjoyment. At least everybody that I knew used it for those reasons, at first. And I knew a lot of people from all walks of life. But yet they were using drugs! Cocaine or heroin—both were really popular back then.

It was my junior year and we had a tough football team, a rather large team in terms of numbers of players. We had over fifty participants competing at the varsity level, and I was the only underclassmen to be in the starting lineup. In fact, I started both ways—as a running back on the offense and a cornerback on the defense. I was the only junior playing; everybody else was a senior. I only came off the field for the kickoff team, and that was only to get a breather if we scored a touchdown or a field goal. I remember we were playing our crosstown rivals, the Waukegan East Bulldogs, and they were stacked. They had a good record that year and they had talent all over the field. We knew we were in for a dog fight against our rivals. It was a very intense game.

I used the football field to get my name out there in my city. I was in the end zone three times—that's three touchdowns. I also had two interceptions and made a bunch of plays that had the public address announcer constantly saying my name, "Doug Harrington." I was just making plays but it got to the point that I was tired of hearing him say my name, Doug Harrington.

One day I was sitting at home in our music studio and I realized that I still had the key to the storage room. I had become curious if the key still fit, so I went to go check it out and it did still fit! I immediately started plotting and scheming and before you know it, I was getting some back and my helmet cleaned in the school. It was crazy! I had different students meet me by the cafeteria at a certain time, or I would get a restroom pass from my teacher and slide by their room, giving them the signal. Then they too got a restroom pass from their teacher and joined me in the storage closet for about ten or fifteen minutes. You'd be amazed at how many girls I was able to manipulate back then. If I were to name the names of the participants cleaning my helmet back then you would be shocked, or you wouldn't believe me. I didn't discriminate either. I had girls that were honor students yet super freaks in that little room. I entertained in that little room my junior and senior year at least twice a week. Sometimes it would happen more than that.

I was a highly recruited football player and received several offers from Division I schools. I wanted to graduate, have a successful college football career and play professional football too. I felt the pressure to succeed because the city had produced many great athletes before me. Some graduated from college, but most of them didn't. In fact, the majority of athletes didn't do well and dropped out of school. I didn't want to be like them.

I remember we were hooping against Highland Park High School, and they were in the sole position of first place at the time. Waukegan East was one game back out of first place, and we were a solid third place in the conference standings behind Highland Park and Waukegan East. The game was the last game of the season before regionals. Regionals was the first bracket of games for schools in the same particular area in the Illinois High School Association. This was also the first time in my entire life that my mom wasn't going to be at the game. I didn't know how I would perform; I just really wanted to make her proud of me.

They had one player on the other team who was a bona fide superstar. I was assigned to guard him. I recall picking him up on a fast break about midcourt, only to be crossed up and hear the oohs and ahhs of the crowd as I was getting up off the floor. The crowd was very unruly. They were throwing dog biscuits at us the entire game and the officials acted like they didn't see them! They even had on Central Suburban League Champion T-shirts. As the game went on, we were getting blown out until one of our players got hot. He started hitting jump shot after jump shot, and single handedly brought us back into the game. Too bad we didn't have the three-point line back then. I remember it was the fourth quarter with eight seconds left in the game. There was a jump ball at our free throw line. We called a timeout to diagram a play. It was drawn up so that the ball would be tipped directly to our hot man and he would take the last shot.

I'll never forget their fans singing the "Na" song—a song made famous by the Chicago White Sox fans, who sing it after every home victory. Our big man tipped the ball directly to our hot man but defense swarmed all over him, preventing him from getting a shot off, so he passed it to me. I was deep in the left corner on the left side of the court. I knew I didn't have much time to get the shot off. So I caught the pass, took one dribble, and let it fly! The shot was in slow motion to me. It went through the rim—nothing but net—and our crowd erupted in cheers. I was immediately mobbed by my teammates and fans as I hit the game winner at the buzzer!

The Highland Park fans were shocked. One of my homeboys hugged me and grabbed me tightly and said to me in my ear something that I'd rather not repeat. I was interviewed by the *Waukegan News Sun* and the *Chicago Tribune* as I told them we wanted to win the game so that Waukegan East could get a share of the title, and we would get second place. I then went on to say that so-and-so stopped by my crib to wish us luck, when in reality a couple of guys from both teams met at my crib and we went into the studio and freestyled and smoked some skunk weed! The newspaper had posted four pictures from the game in the sports section, and I was in every picture. As you read the article, you will see he had twenty-eight points. He killed me and I had only ten points, but I had the game winner!

CHAPTER 8
Class of 1986

My senior year was a trip. We would be downstairs in our basement studio for hours making music, snorting cocaine, and smoking primos. For those of you that don't know, a primo is a cigarette laced with cocaine. The smell was minty but the high was intense. I noticed back then that I wasn't very creative under the influence, and I couldn't play any musical instruments like normal when I was under the influence. We would meet up, get high, and just sing and rap to previously recorded music. This would happen at least once a week. It was nothing for us to go through several packs of coke that measured in the amount of a sixteenth of a gram. To those that are unfamiliar, it was about a hundred dollars a pack, and we never paid for anything!

Ya see, I had friends in what were considered high places. My guys supplied all of Lake County and parts of Kenosha County with cocaine. I had access to drugs free of charge, basically whenever I wanted them. I remember rolling to the southside of Chicago in this rundown neighborhood. There was trash everywhere, no grass, and broken bottles scattered all over the place. It was really sad. We pulled up to the back of this three-story building and went upstairs to the top floor. We knocked at the door and this thick fine sista opened the door and let us in. And oh, my God, I thought we were at the Ritz-Carlton someplace. I mean, the inside had plush carpet, leather furniture, a big screen television, artwork on the walls—it was too clean! We were there to pick up a kilo of cocaine with a street value unheard of. Despite this distraction I still managed to stay focused on football.

There were five Division I schools still in the running for my services: the University of Illinois, Illinois State University, Northern Illinois University, University of Minnesota, and Iowa State University. I had visited three of the schools, and each one was offering me a full athletic scholarship. But they all wanted me to attend William Rainey Harper College, a junior college, to help me get my grade point average up because the NCAA was instituting this new rule called Proposition 48. It was a rule stating all players must maintain a 2.0 grade point average to be eligible to play. I did just enough in high school, so I never really paid attention to my grade point average. My grade point average was a 2.1 at the time, so it was either sit out for a season—meaning redshirt—or attend Harper Junior College for two years. Those were my final two options, and I had no intention of sitting on the sidelines.

I recall we were scheduled to play against Niles West but they had a teachers' strike in Niles Township. North Chicago was scheduled to play against Niles North. Now both schools were in different conferences, and different divisions, but both of our opponents were under the same teachers' strike in Niles Township. The higher-ups in our school district and North Chicago School District got together and agreed that we would play against each other. They made it official that we would play North Chicago on their field on Saturday instead of Niles West.

Now, North Chicago was the next town over from Waukegan going south. We knew them very well and they knew us. We played against them a couple of times before high school and, I must admit, they had some ballers on their team. The high school was known for their track program and having fine girls. Their boys' track program had just won the Illinois High School Association State Track and Field Championship. Their relay team was also their starting secondary, so they had some speed.

I also noticed they had plenty of girls in attendance at the football game. I recall the second play of the game. Our coach called my favorite play, thirty-four crossbuck. I took the handoff and scampered forty-eight yards right up the middle of the field, untouched, to the end zone for a touchdown! My guy talks about that particular play all the time. He asks me how I outran them, when they were all faster than me and they had the angle too. "How did you do this?" I was asked. So I let him know that they had track speed and I had game speed, and there was a difference. You have to have played the game before to know what I'm really talking about.

I found the end zone one more time, to go with my two interceptions, as we defeated the North Chicago Warhawks. I found out that a lot of the girls in North Chicago were ready to give up some back and clean my helmet! So me being me, I let them! My senior year was crazy for me. I was voted the "Most Athletic" at my high school. I wore two knee pads and two thigh pads to make myself look bigger to my opponents. The game program had me listed at 185 pounds, though in reality, I was closer to 150 pounds soaking wet.

I had my mind set on going to Harper Junior College and then to the Illinois State or the University of Minnesota. I knew that I had the talent and skills to go to a Division I school. This was obviously apparent when I played at the All-Star Game.

It was a game that featured a bunch of All-State players from Illinois. I showed out at this game. I know that my mom and my coach were very proud of me after this game! I had two interceptions to go along with multiple tackles. I even ran back a punt sixty-seven yards in which I should have scored. I did all of this against top notch Division I competition. I should've won the All-Star Game Most Valuable Player Award. They ended up giving the award to our quarterback, who had two touchdown passes in the game, but I made sure that everyone who was in attendance knew who Harrington was.

After the game I remember riding home and having this conversation with my mom. She was afraid that if I went to school locally at Harper that I would get caught up with my friends, or just be a number if I attended one of the bigger Division I schools and I wouldn't graduate. Midland University was a smaller school that made me a full scholarship offer and the opportunity to play right away and not attend junior college, plus I would get the help I needed from the professors to graduate.

My mom then challenged me. She basically challenged me to be a man and step out on faith. I really didn't know what faith was at the time, but I didn't want to be just a number at a big school and not graduate because the class was big and the professor didn't really know me—he would only know that I played football. So I talked to my coach. He was also one of my teachers. He told me that he thought I had a better chance of graduating from Midland University in Nebraska. I did understand they had the teacher-to-student ratio that my mom sought so that I would get the extra help and attention I needed to graduate.

So I took what my mom suggested as a challenge. I was gonna go to a school that I never visited. I knew nothing about the school or the city of Fremont in which it was located. I just wanted to play ball and I knew they wanted me. I eventually went to Midland University in Fremont, Nebraska, and I'm glad I did! God was showing me favor back then. I just didn't know it.

CHAPTER 9
Freshman in College

I got off the plane in Omaha, Nebraska, expecting to see a bunch of cornfields and stuff. The head coach sent some brother to scoop me up from the airport. We talked for a few minutes and I found out that he went to Evanston Township High School. We called it E Town, located right outside of Chicago. He told me what I needed to know about this college I was about to attend. Remember, I didn't visit this place because it was just too late, so I had to milk him for as much information that I could get.

We drove about an hour to the location in Fremont, Nebraska. I didn't know what to expect or what I was in for. I just know my momma told me to go away, have faith, and she would do whatever she could to support me. I knew that she just wanted me to go somewhere I couldn't come home every weekend and get caught up with the wrong crowd. My mom attended every baseball game, every football game, and every basketball game except one. She promised to come see me play at least once a year. She knew what I could do. It was just time for me to man up, cut the umbilical cord, and be on my own.

I was recruited by all colleges as a defensive back, but I just wanted the opportunity to play. The starting secondary at Midland University consisted of two seniors from Washington, D.C., that played the corners and they were tough; a senior strong safety from Chicago who was really big; and a hard-hitting junior free safety who was also from the Washington, D.C., area. These brothers were strong. I mean, physically strong. I knew that I had to be on top of my game if I had any chance of getting playing time, let alone a starting job, or I could be the first defensive back called in passing situations.

35

College football was tougher than I thought. We practiced three times a day: early in the morning, in the afternoon, and during the evening. We were going at it at every session, and I began to climb my way up the depth chart. I remember our first scrimmage. For those of you that don't know what a scrimmage is, it's a practice against your teammates in game-like conditions. My number was called earlier. I was number twenty-four, and not my favorite number twenty-three. The number twenty-three was given to a running back and he just happened to redshirt, meaning miss that entire season.

I had the opportunity to go against the first team offense and I was hyped up. I was matched up against our starting wide receiver who was six-foot-four and a solid 195 pounds from Rich South High School, another school in the Chicago area known for producing good football players. He was fast too, so I had to respect his speed. He ran an out pattern, and the quarterback was on point. There was nothing I could do but ride him out of bounds as the official hollered first down. The offense ran a few more running plays in the other direction and up the middle. Then I guess they wanted to pick on the freshman—me. I didn't know it, but I was ready for them. We were in cover one and I had to contain responsibility. The quarterback dropped back to pass and the big receiver ran an out again, only this time it was time to make a play as I baited the quarterback. He thought the receiver was open and threw the pass. That's when I jumped the route. I stepped in front of the receiver and intercepted the ball. I was headed in the opposite direction to the end zone for a touchdown! Later, I was back deep to receive a punt and returned the seventy-three yards to the end zone for another touchdown.

My teammates were showing me love and respect as a true freshman. They knew that this little kid could play. The coaches were impressed too. Later that evening the head coach met with me in his office and said his staff were thinking of ways they could get me on the field to help this football team. He asked me, "How would you feel about playing wide receiver?"

I didn't even think about it. I said, "Yeah, I will play it." I just wanted a chance to play! So they gave me a white jersey, number twenty-four; that's what color the offense wore. I already had an orange jersey, number twenty-four, the color of our defense. I could do nothing but say, *Wow, I was still going both ways!* In Waukegan, I was a cornerback and running back. Now I was a cornerback and a wide receiver. Here we go again. It was crazy! Here I am, scheming with these guys on defense trying to take the receiver's head off. Now I'm running across the middle and those same guys I was scheming with are now trying to take my head off! It was really crazy.

I never really thought about it, as in playing a wide receiver. Like I said, I just wanted to play, which brings me to the hardest I ever been hit on the field in all of my years of playing football. You see, we didn't have all these new rules like defenseless receivers or crowning. I recall I was coming across the middle. I was trying to make a name for myself and beat out the starting receiver and impress the coaches. I was trying to show off my talent and skills. The quarterback's pass was intended for me but it was high. I jumped and leaped high in the air when I was partially hit by our free safety. He immediately told me, "Shorty, don't you go across the middle like that again. I could've fucked you up!" I realized not only did he pull up on me, he only hit half of my body! Yet, you could hear the collision. As I proceeded to try get myself off the ground and walk back to the huddle, my legs wouldn't move. I got really scared! I was also trying to play it off. So I stood there and I reached down to grab my socks and pulled them up, and they were already up. I took a deep breath, and began to walk back to the huddle. It was a scary experience for me.

Our starting receiver got hurt in practice and I ended up being the starting wide receiver, a position that I'd never played before. I was a starter in my first collegiate game. I also played on the kickoff team in my first game. We were playing against Northwestern College in Iowa. It was in the fourth quarter and I ran a simple slant route, broke a tackle, and I was gone sixty-four yards to the end zone for a touchdown!

I ended up reaching the end zone only four times my freshman year. I was still wearing two knee pads and two thigh pads to make me look bigger and absorb the punishment. I knew I had to get bigger and stronger to compete. I was the only freshman to start on offense. We had this one guy on our defensive line that was pretty tough. He was a freshman too.

Things on the field were going pretty nice for me. Things off the field were going pretty nice for me too. The women at the school were slow by our city standards, I thought. They were cleaning my helmet at an unbelievable pace. I was shocked. I thought to myself, *They are backwards out here. They will clean your helmet before giving up the back.* I wasn't used to being treated this way, but I wasn't complaining—I was loving every minute of it!

After the football season came to an end, I gathered together a group of freshmen football players to play intramural basketball. We were all freshmen, so I came up with the name the Fresh Crew. This intramural league was tough. Athletes from every sport were participating. We won the intramural basketball championship three out of four years. I also created a rap group called the School Boyz. We won the school talent show three out of four years and were blessed with a trip to the world famous Apollo Theater in Brooklyn, New York. I will tell you about that later.

My professors were giving me the extra help that I knew I needed to be successful in the classroom and my grades were good. The grade point average was coming up. I had the love and respect of my teammates, and women were cleaning my helmet daily. I was smoking weed whenever I wanted. Life was great!

CHAPTER 10

Crazy Year

S ophomore year was rough but it was a productive season. I worked hard during the off season. I put on some weight and I'd gotten stronger. I also switched from wide receiver to running back, my natural position. I had put on enough weight so that I could endure the hits and the punishment delivered by our opponents. Last season, I admit, I just wasn't big enough to perform at the collegiate level. There were some big ole boys we were up against. I was also able to talk to my teammate into giving me the number twenty-three, my old high school number. Now, I can't remember how many carries or yards I had. Those that know me know I'm bad with numbers. However, I do know that I led the team in rushing yardage and scoring that season!

I did enough to earn NIAC honors as a sophomore (that's the Nebraska Intercollegiate Athletic Conference First Team). The last person to accomplish this feat as a sophomore was named Don Beebe, and he was playing on Sundays for the Buffalo Bills. We went on to play a playoff game that season, similar to a bowl game for NCAA schools. I recall flying up there to Seattle, Washington, to play Pacific Lutheran University. We played a good game but we didn't play our best. We ended up losing. However, I did reach the end zone on my favorite play, the crossbuck between the railroads. In other words, I ran up the middle of the field in between my two guys for a touchdown.

As my popularity had grown on and off campus, I remember going with one of my teammates to a party in his hometown, a very small town. You should've seen the looks I got. Man, we had fun, but it was also an experience. The party was held inside a barn. Yeah, you read it right, a barn! We were getting glares

and stares to where we came to our own conclusion that these people had never before been in the presence of black people before. They may have seen African Americans or black folks on television, but this was the real deal in the flesh.

My friends and I began to mingle and interact with the partygoers, knowing that we were being watched. We were on our best behavior. We were drinking beer and dancing a bit when I was approached by this woman who wanted to know if the myth about black men was true. After a few more drinks from the keg of beer, I was then led out the door and behind the barn. Once we were back there, she didn't waste any time in cleaning my helmet, and she was convinced the myth was true.

I started to realize that something ain't right with me. I began to find myself fantasizing about getting my helmet cleaned. I then created a challenge for myself. *How many times can I get some back or my helmet cleaned in one day?* I wondered. I then was on a mission. I could go into details but it would take all day and possibly would expose those who were involved. The truth being told, it happened to me seven times! That's right, seven times in one day! Now I know my haters and non-believers think I'm just making this stuff up to make myself look good. I wish I was making this stuff up. I swear to you everything I'm telling you is the truth. I realize that I had a problem and didn't know who to get help from, but I didn't even want help. I knew I never forced myself on women or made them do something against their will. I realized that I was just addicted to the sexual act and didn't care who I hurt in the process. I was living, what I thought, was the good life, both on and off the field.

I recall this little woman was hanging out down the hallway with her friends visiting my teammates. She came to my room and asked me about our sign, a sign that read "Beware of the Blackhole." The Blackhole was a dead-end hallway with three rooms occupied by black students. "Once you go in, you don't come out" was our motto! After she heard our motto, she began flirting with me anyway. She told me her name, but all I remember was she had an awesome body and looked like Madonna, and she was a virgin!

We talked a few hours about everything, from classes, cars, and sports to racism and sex—you name it, we talked about it. We were on the subject of sex when we started kissing. One thing led to another and before you knew it she started cleaning my helmet. I was able to convince her to let me be her first. She put a condom on me and was ready to ride! I was kind and gentle and she ended up staying all night. Once the morning had come and all the alcohol had worn off, she quickly gathered her clothes and belongings and was out the door. She was gone and I didn't even get her number.

A few days had passed when I noticed a message on my answering machine. I listened to the message and it was a detective from the Fremont Police Department. He wanted to speak with me and said it was imperative that I call him and set up a meeting. I was scared as hell, y'all. I had no one I could talk to. My girl at the time was better known to me as "The Pitcher's Mound." She really knew me but I couldn't confide anything to her because I was guilty of cheating with someone else. Knowing that I'm a young black man in an all-white town, they were gonna try to hang me for whatever reason. I called him to set up a meeting, but he gave me no clue as to what it was about and why he wanted to talk to meet me.

I went to the Fremont Police Station. They had me in a little room just like on the television show *The First 48*. He asked me a few questions about a particular night then he showed me a picture. It was that little Madonna look-alike! The detective told me she was screaming out rape and I didn't understand why. After I began to explain to the detective in detail the events of that night, I left that little room even more scared than when I had entered. I got her number from that friend she was originally visiting that stayed down the hall. I immediately went to my dorm room and called her and there was no answer. I had never forced myself on anyone, let alone take me some back. I didn't have to. I had women who acted like they were angels. As soon as they were away from their friends they turned into porn stars.

I found out that her dad discovered she lost her virginity to a black man and he was out to get me! I think it was my statement that she put the condom on me that really helped me. I assume she told him the same because no charges were ever filed. She would later call me trying to explain, and I told her to lose my number as I hung up the phone. I dodged a bullet knowing that I just got myself out of a situation, not realizing God blessed me and removed me from that situation.

CHAPTER 11
Junior and Senior Year

Junior and senior year went by too fast. I did enter the end zone twenty more times within these two seasons. I finished my career entering the end zone a total of thirty-six times. I was BMOC, or the Big Man on Campus. I had my girl I called "The Pitcher's Mound," and she was sexing me up every night—and I do mean every night. I was enjoying it too. There were women who acted like they didn't even know me as they saw me at different locations throughout the campus. These same women were inviting me to their houses or dorm rooms after hours and cleaning my helmet all while keeping the sexual relationship quiet so their friends wouldn't know that they were screwing a black guy. It was crazy! Some of my teammates were excited to be involved with women I had already and moved on. It was crazy, I tell ya!

Finals were approaching real soon and I needed to have good grades in every classroom if I were to continue to raise my grade point average and stay on pace for graduation. My brother and sisters had all gone to college, but none of them graduated for various reasons. I wanted to be the first in our family to graduate from college. I had also talked to my agent who informed me that some NFL scouts wanted me and a teammate to perform for them. God was blessing me way back then, but I didn't even know it.

I'll admit I had no clue about God. I didn't have a relationship with Him back then. I do know that I had a passion for music, which was evident to me every time I returned home. I was quick to record some beats and instrumentals that I could take back with me to school. I would use these tracks to freestyle too. I was goofing around and I made this track, and a member of my rap group called the School Boyz really liked it. I thought the track was easy, basic, and generic. To make a long story short, I created a song off this generic-sounding kiddie keyboard, and I added this hook to the beat and the song "She's My Baby" was created. The song was talking about a member of our group's daughter. He liked it so much he took the instrumental background version back home with him to the Washington, D.C., area and entered it into a *Star Search* competition. He did this without any of us knowing he did. He was a last minute contestant on a D.C. *Star Search* and he won first place. Remember, I wasn't too fond of this particular song. I had created many songs I thought that had more dynamics and substance at the time. Well, he won first place and all the first place winners were awarded a trip to the world famous Apollo Theater!

I was excited that a song I wrote and produced was under the spotlight. He told us that he knew he had a hit and really needed the rest of the group in order to win, so we started to prepare for our performance at the Apollo when I noticed the date was around the same time that we had our finals. I double-checked, and they were the exact same day! I had to talk to my professors and see if I could take my final tests early. Some agreed to give me my test early, some disagreed. I didn't really like my situation as I was forced to make a decision, so I stayed. Somehow, the local newspaper, *The Fremont Tribune*, found out about our trip to the Apollo. They wanted to do a story about it. They didn't know that I wasn't going because of finals. Lord knows I wanted to go. Once they found out that I wasn't going and why, they ran with the story and placed it right on the front page and it read "Rapper Chooses Studies Over Apollo," making me look like I was studying but in reality I was really mad that I wasn't going!

I knew I was at Midland for my fifth year. The majority of the student athletes took five years to graduate, so I was cool with that. I was an assistant coach on the football team in charge of the running backs and the return teams. The football season went by quickly, and it was hoop season before you knew it. I had gotten with my friend who was a pool shark, and together we coached the traveling boys' basketball team, which was a great experience of teaching and coaching. I recall, since we were traveling, some of the little towns we were going to had never seen a black man in the flesh. We decided to be clean and wear a tie with our attire to every game. We were clean too! We endured some racism along the way. It was obvious to us that some people were just plain ignorant. And being me, I began getting my helmet cleaned by some of my players' parents. It was at this time that God began to show me more favor. I just didn't know it.

There was this major teachers' fair happening at the University of Nebraska and our entire education department was encouraged to attend. I didn't really want to go. My resume was incomplete; my focus was not there. I was looking for every excuse in the book not to go. Then I ran into my professor. He insisted that I go pass out a few resumes and work on my interviewing skills, so I reluctantly took his advice and attended the job fair. At this point I'm an education major, and there were school districts from all over the country attending the fair. You name it, they were there: from New York, Chicago, Philadelphia, New Mexico, California, Houston, and Colorado to name a few. They were all school districts ready to hire.

I walked around observing my environment and chose Houston first because I had family there with my sister. Plus, I'd visited that city's college, Texas Southern University, during a college tour of Historically Black Colleges and Universities (HBCUs). I gave the lady representing the Houston Independent School District my resume. She interviewed me, asking me a few questions and BAM! She offered me a job! I was as surprised as anyone. I couldn't believe it. I had a job waiting on me and I hadn't even graduated yet. God was blessing me and I didn't even know it.

I went to another school district's table, one in California, and I was to try my luck again, not knowing that I just received a blessing from God! This one was in Bakersfield, California, to be exact. I walked up to the table, took a look around, then handed the representative my resume and proceeded to answer his questions. As he was conducting his interview, he looked at me and he offered me a job too! I couldn't believe it! I was two for two.

As the news begins to spread, my peers were hating and stuff. There were so many of us attending the job fair, and I'm sure everyone knew about it, but only a few congratulated me or wished me good luck. Now I wasn't smarter or sharper than some of my peers, yet I was the only one offered two jobs. We had close to a hundred people at this job fair. I'm sure they were shocked that I was leaving the job fair with a job! Just think—I wasn't even planning on attending!

CHAPTER 12
Mother's Day Weekend 1991

There was plenty for me to get excited about. It was Mother's Day weekend and I was about to graduate and receive a bachelor of arts degree in education. I also had a tryout with the Pittsburgh Steelers of the National Football League. Life was treating me well. I was very happy with myself and the progress that I'd made living on my own. It wasn't long ago I felt challenged and I rose to the occasion and met that challenge. Now it was time for me to enjoy my commitment and all my hard work.

I was finally gonna graduate from college. As I walked across that stage feeling proud of my accomplishments at Midland University, my family, my teammates, my friends, and my peers were all in attendance. I had also talked to my agent, who was also in attendance, and he told me the Pittsburgh Steelers were still very interested in me, so after graduation I got me a plane ticket and I was off to St. Joseph College in Latrobe, Pennsylvania, the site of OTAs (organized team activities). I was about to fulfill a lifelong dream with an opportunity to play in the NFL. The head coach was Chuck Knoll and his coordinators were Tom Moore on offense and Bill Cowher on defense. I was number seven, or dead last, on the depth chart so I had my work cut out for me. Their starting running back was Barry Foster, and Tim Worley was the backup. Those two were a lock to be on the team, so in reality it was five guys fighting for one position—one spot on the team. I was six-one, 223 pounds. I ran a 4.5 in the forty-yard dash. I bench pressed 225 pounds over twenty times. I'm not sure what my vertical jump was. I don't remember, but I could slam dunk a basketball, so there was no doubt that I met their physical qualifications.

Of the other four cats I was competing against, not one had any defensive experience, so I knew I had to get my shine on through my special teams play to make this team. I was doing me and making plays in practice, working my way up the charts with my special teams play. My running back skills were evident. If I were to say I had a weakness, it would be my pass blocking. It was something I just wasn't asked to do a great deal in college, so I wasn't really used to it. We were on the ropes doing this drill, something I had done many, many times before. Then it happened! This particular time my left leg slid in the mud and I fell awkwardly. When I got up, there was a sharp pain in my hip. I never felt pain like this before. The pain was worse than being stood up at the line of scrimmage and gang tackled, so I reluctantly went to go see a trainer and had him look at it. He took a look and immediately scheduled me for an MRI.

Throughout my entire career I had never had an injury before. Now, I've been hurt before, but as a team player you learn to play hurt. This was different. I couldn't do what was natural for me, the D-smooth cross step, a move where I manipulate my shoulders but my lower body remains square. This was my signature move and I couldn't do it anymore without there being pain! The trainer suggested that I rest my body. I was in shock. *Rest!* I thought. I was a free agent and I had to prove myself to the staff and my teammates if I was gonna make the team. What did he mean, rest? This was an opportunity of a lifetime. I would rest later. What the hell was he talking about, rest!

Well, I was put on their "physically unable to perform" list the next day. I went to get the MRI done. The doctor told me that I had strained a hip muscle that would require rest. I couldn't believe it. I was sick. All of my dreams of playing in the NFL were gone! I was cut the next day. I was told by the trainer to stick around if I could; he wanted to monitor my hip. I was granted permission to travel with the team for the remainder of the preseason. I guess the training staff was using me as their guinea pig to monitor my hip as a practice run for the upcoming season—I don't know. I do know that the eight-week training camp had come to an end, and I was invited to a birthday bash for one of the players at the Hyatt Regency in Harrisburg. I attended the party that was filled with drinks, all kinds of party favors, and escorts. I ended up with an escort, went to a room, and got my helmet cleaned.

God had given me a chance to experience NFL life. He knew I would have probably been kicked out of the league for a failed drug test. I still had it pretty bad when it came to weed and it wasn't legal anywhere at that time. After the party was over, I went back to my dorm room and gathered all my belongings and I ended up flying to Houston, Texas, and staying at my sister's house for a while. A letter arrived from Pittsburgh stating my conditioning was why I was released. Lord knows my hip was through. I thought I was in good shape! I knew why it was over.

Well, I was in H-Town, ready to start my teaching job. I did give football a shot again and tried out with the Houston Oilers, but the pain I felt just trying to do my signature move was crazy. Over a period of time, my sister and I weren't seeing eye to eye on some things, so I moved to my guy's house and he had two Technic 1200 turntables, which brought me back to my days as a disc jockey. He also reintroduced me to cocaine, Texas-style!

CHAPTER 13

Coach Harrington

I was at Hamilton Middle School teaching and coaching girls' basketball and girls' track. I was able to negotiate a high school football coaching deal instead of the coaching at the middle school. God was showing me favor because at the time this wasn't happening. I was at Scarborough High School coaching football plus my duties at Hamilton. Now, the girls' basketball team hadn't won a game in five years. In fact, the principal told me she just wanted someone to work with them—they had no expectations to win. When we won our first game of the season, it was like we won the NBA Championship! They were jumping and running around the gym celebrating and stuff and I didn't understand it. I *expected* to win! I remember my lunch period and my planning period were back-to-back, so I had almost two hours of free time every day. They had a McDonald's restaurant located right next door, so I would go and order a large vanilla shake, then stop by my guy's crib and get twenty dollars' worth of cocaine, sometimes on credit. Then I would go to one of my students' houses and get high with his mom, as she would clean my helmet. I did this routine every day!

Yeah, I was ho or whatever you wanna call me. I was addicted to sex and the cocaine just added to it. It enhanced it. See, cocaine is a stimulant. It motivates and stimulates the opposite sex. It also enhances your five senses: your taste, sight, hearing, touch, and smell. It was hard to identify those who were functional addicts because they looked like your everyday people but they just chose to use for whatever reason. A lot of people don't know cocaine was used as medication back in the 1930s. Research it if you don't believe me. I remember a friend

51

of mine would say, "For every health problem or issue, there is a pill for help or relief." For high blood pressure, there was a pill one would take. For headaches, there was a pill; for sinus issues, there was a pill. We had a sickness and cocaine was our pill!

I remember I was coaching my girls' basketball team, and my assistant I hired was also a good friend. It was the fourth quarter and we were up by twenty points. We were on the bench trying to figure out how I was gonna avoid the four women I had at the game. I had my girl, the nurse, a teacher's aide, and a parent all in the gym at one time! I recall I would go upstairs to my office, smoke a primo, then come downstairs and shake hands with the principal and then go and teach my class. Now that I think about it, that's crazy! I did this for years. Now, my girls are cool. I used to tell them all the time to hook me up with your momma or your auntie and they did. It was crazy I had women at my disposal.

Anyway, most of my basketball team also ran track for me. I didn't know much about track and field. The girls ran and ran for Coach Harrington though. We would go on to win the City of Houston Middle School Track and Field Championship. We were the best in the city. That was equivalent to winning the Chicago Public League Championship. My assistant was also my homeboy and he knew I got high. I remember calling the teacher's aide who was my lady at the time. I misdialed her number, but I can hear her conversation. Instead of dialing 9989 I dialed 9999 by accident. I was able to hear the entire conversation, and it was my assistant coach talking to my lady. He was trying his best to make a move with her. I was confused. I was either high tripping or I was right.

Now, I had a lot of women in my life up to this point. There was something about her other than that kung fu grip that had me whooped. I couldn't figure it out. I confronted them both and they denied it. He was like, "Man, you need to slow down with that cocaine." I thought I was just high tripping and for two weeks I really thought I was tripping. Then she came to me confessing that he was trying to talk to her and everything I said was true. It messed my head up even more. I didn't know what was what.

Months passed, and then the highlight of my life or the greatest day in my life occurred! The birth of my daughter DaQuoiya Janae Harrington gave me this joy that I just can't speak into words! I called her Coco. I thought that my baby would have something wrong with her based upon my sexual history. She turned out to be a beautiful, happy child and I was a proud papa!

CHAPTER 14

Stab Wounds

I got married in spite of knowing I had an addiction problem that I hid from my family. I was set up to fail no matter what. It was my fault, yet she stayed with me, enduring all of my BS. And to make matters worse, I had another problem too that I needed to address. I was stealing out of stores in spite of being financially blessed. It was called kleptomania or something like that. I didn't understand it, but I had it. I knew that I would steal some stuff from a store or a convenience store. It didn't matter. I would have the money right in my pocket, yet I would steal a forty-five-cent candy bar or whatever insignificant thing. I was stealing, which I knew I was wrong. But I chose to do it anyway. It gave me a feeling or a rush that I only got when I was on the football field. I couldn't figure out if it was the act of not getting caught or the cameras focused on me. I didn't understand what was happening with me. I had the money to buy whatever, but I would take it anyway. I just stole it for that rush. That feeling, it's indescribable!

I recall when my family was going to New Light Baptist Church for choir rehearsal, I was going to the dope house to get me some cocaine. It was crazy! I finally said to myself, *I know I can do better than this*. I knew that I could make the choir sound better. They already sounded good with the drummer, organist, and the choir that they had in place. I knew I could enhance their sound and make it sound even better. It was the commitment that bothered me. The reverend was invited to somebody's church for service every Sunday. Wherever he went, he had his two-piece band right there with him, along with every choir member, so it was a huge commitment on my part.

I couldn't bear to watch an NFL game. I was still getting over the fact that I was just there but failed! So I wasn't really missing anything. I just knew I had to do something to keep me occupied and focused. And music was something I could do and not worry about getting high. As long as I was playing my bass guitar, I knew I wasn't trying to get high, get me some back, get my helmet cleaned, or run up in some store just to get my adrenaline fix. I decided I would playing my bass guitar for the church.

Music was a way for me to stay occupied and fight back against my addictions, but I was playing for the church for the wrong reason. Playing at the church, I was having fun. I was really vibing with the drummer. We constantly played some hip hop underscores. Quiet as it is kept. My pastor told me, "Doug, we can only offer you this amount right now, but you're very good and there will be other churches who will hear you play and offer you more!"

Now, I was unaware of the financial aspect of this part of the church. I even declined the money the church was offering me. Then the pastor called me into his office and explained to me with scripture why I was getting paid, so I accepted the financial blessing and used the funds to support my family dining at different restaurants after service. It became routine that we went out to eat after service. My pastor was right. I received several different offers to play and for much more money at different churches throughout the Houston area.

I'd made a commitment to myself and to my family to stay involved with the music ministry at the New Light Baptist Church. I did join the choir and began playing the bass guitar for the First Baptist Church and their weekly financial blessing along with New Light Baptist Church, which was enough money for me to pay the monthly mortgage payment on our house. If I was playing music in my free time, then I wasn't getting high. I was still a functional addict trying desperately to stop. These were the best years of my life! I was happy just enjoying life, and doing the right thing. This was how God meant for me to live, although I was fighting my demons. It was tough for me.

I remember going to a friend's room to do what we do, and that was getting high. I'd called my connection and we both had spent the same amount of money and received the same amount of drugs. I taught myself how to get my dope, make it last longer, and spend less money. For example, we both brought a twenty dollar rock of cocaine. We both had approximately the same amount, only he broke his down into four pieces and I broke mine down into eight pieces. We were smoking good. Then he got upset because I was still getting high long after him. He had smoked all of his. He started to look at me all crazy. He thought I was holding out on him and I had received more. He began to question me, one thing led to another, and before I knew it he swung at me and the punch landed right on my jaw!

I gathered myself and proceeded to kick his ass. He was picking himself off the floor when he grabbed a knife in the process. We continued to fight as I was able to squeeze out the door. I thought I was sweating but realized it was blood and I'd been stabbed! I then proceeded to get high with the remainder of my dope before I called for an ambulance to assist me. When I think about it now, I realize how crazy that was. I felt I was fine but I wanted to be sure. After being examined and X-rayed, the doctor said I was okay. If the knife he had stuck me an inch higher, it would have punctured my heart. I called it lucky at the time, but I know now it was God!

CHAPTER 15
Shots Fired

I was at this crib getting high and getting my helmet cleaned when I noticed this dude kept leaving then coming back with money all day long. I was curious as to what he was doing to get money. So I asked him and he volunteered to show me his lick. For those that don't know, a lick was a fast way to get money. He went into a grocery store and came running out with a handheld basket full of stuff. An employee of the store was chasing behind him as we drove off. He would later take me to his fence. Now, a fence was someone who would purchase the stolen items for cash. Normally, it was half of the sticker price. He later told me he got a dollar per item, and he had thirty-five items. I told him he was working too hard and not smart with all of that running and stuff. So he called me out, and I showed him the very next day.

We got ready to go. I had on some comfortable shoes, dress pants, a polo shirt, a hat, and some glasses. I also had a pen and a clipboard. I walked into the store with confidence as if I worked for the company. I grabbed a shopping cart and went directly to the back of the building where the sign read "Employees Only." I quickly located a box and placed it inside of the shopping cart. I then went to the aisle with the medication and with one sweeping motion I cleared the entire shelf into the box. It took me all but two or three minutes total. I then proceeded to go out of the store acting like I was an employee of a company doing a recall.

We then took the box to his fence. I watched him count 427 items! He gave me $300 and I had to come back to get my $127 later in the afternoon. I was told he didn't have enough money at the store. This activity went on daily for months. Once the stores caught on, we had to try something different. I was hitting different stores and different malls throughout the day. I was high and confident that I could walk in any store in the U.S. with nothing and walk out with cash and merchandise, and in a bag with a receipt—I was that good! I had drug dealers meeting me back at my hotel room after placing orders and getting a firsthand look at my merchandise. I had everything from Tommy Hilfiger designer clothes to Nike Air Jordans—top-of-the-line merchandise.

There was one incident in which I'd called up a drug dealer friend and told him what I wanted, as I was making a large purchase. I began to wait for him and minutes turned into hours. After waiting several hours, and making several phone calls, I decided I was tired of waiting, so I went to make a purchase somewhere else. When I was gone, the individual that I was waiting hours for finally arrived at my room looking for me. This helmet cleaner I had waiting in my room let him in my room. She just wanted some cocaine! When he realized I wasn't there, he tried on my hat that I'd left on my bed along with a matching Tommy Hilfiger shirt and short set. He then left my room with my hat on his head. I later returned to my room and noticed that my hat was missing. I was told that he finally stopped by. I then proceeded to get me some back and get my helmet cleaned.

A few hours passed when looked out the window and noticed my friend's car was right outside. He had the drop top Mustang 5.0 with the big shiny rims and all that! He also still had on my Tommy Hilfiger hat from my room—I still had the matching shirt and shorts. He was well-known as "The Man," as he sold cocaine and had several clients. He and I had a few words with each other because he took all day to get there, and I told him that nobody could dictate or tell me how to spend my money! He was high off that wet (marijuana dipped in embalming fluid) and drunk off that syrup (liquid Tylenol with codeine). I thought I knew him pretty well but he was mad at me because I'd shopped and made a large purchase from another dealer.

Again, I let him know that he doesn't dictate who and where I spent my money! "I waited a few hours and you never showed up! What else was I supposed to do?" I asked him.

Then I asked him to give me my hat back, which he just happened to have on his head. He responded by telling me that he wasn't giving me shit, as he called me a punk ass nigga from Chicago! There were people standing outside and on the balcony leaning over the railings he was trying to impress. I then challenged him and said, "Get out of that car and I will show you a punk ass nigga from Chicago!"

He got out of the car and I whooped his ass all up and down the parking lot. He was trying to make himself look good, but I embarrassed him. Remember, I'm the user and he was the big-time drug dealer. He then jumped in his car as I returned to my room to gather my belongings. I knew he was coming back. Only about five minutes had passed and I could hear the car drive up and stop. As I heard him open the car door, and I could hear different people pleading with him, "Don't do it!" I could hear him walking up the stairs towards my room. I heard all of these things very clearly because I was high.

I didn't know what to do so I hid behind the doorway. I remember saying the words, "Lord help me!" He kicked in my door and headed straight towards the bathroom where he thought I was hiding. I was behind the door next to this long dresser. He saw me and I began to duck and cover as he started to shoot at me. Pow! Pow! Pow! Pow! He then approached me to deliver the kill shot. He aimed the gun directly at my heart. Pow! I later found out that this shot went through my left bicep, but it was one of God's angels that deflected the bullet.

I was able to wrestle the gun away from him as he had gotten too close. I then had total control of his gun. I proceeded to fire his gun at him as he ran out the door. The bullets were all gone! I was trying to get up when my friends came running to my aid. They helped me get up when I noticed my left leg. My foot had turned totally backwards and my thigh was swollen. My thigh was bigger than Newhouse's! (Robert Newhouse was a Dallas Cowboys football player known for his humongous thighs!)

59

As they assisted me to another room, all I could think about was my next hit of cocaine! A friend of mine gave me a twenty-dollar rock. I wanted to numb the pain. I put that whole thing in my pipe and started smoking it. I had never done that before, placing the entire rock of cocaine in my pipe! I could see the paramedics at a distance coming to get me as I was still trying to hit my cocaine. I was aware of one shot that had injured my leg. As the paramedics began to check me out, they could see I had suffered multiple gunshot wounds and called me a potential shock victim as they placed the oxygen mask on me.

I woke up hours later with my family standing around my bed. I was on Fox News and all the news stations. I had been shot five times. Yeah, five times, and I survived! I didn't know that it was God who saved me. I received numerous letters and cards from students throughout the Houston Independent School District. I'd shattered my left femur and I now have a pole in my leg and four screws, two at the top and two at the bottom. I recall that I couldn't go upstairs so I ended up staying at my sister's house. Two detectives came to see me with a photo lineup just like on my favorite show, *The First 48*. I could have very easily been the victim and had my own episode! I selected the individual who was responsible for shooting me. A couple months later he was murdered in New Orleans, but it was about five or six years until I found out about it.

CHAPTER 16

Newlight Records

I had just survived five gunshot wounds. The bullets hit me in each leg and each arm. At the time I thought it was me, but in reality it was God who saved me! I filled out this crime victims' compensation form so I could receive a nice sum of money for missed wages. I received the check and paid some bills and used the remainder to purchase a Roland VS 880 Digital Work-station. It was an expensive piece of equipment back then and it was made to record music. I knew I had to create my own environment similar to the environment my uncles raised me in. I knew that I had a passion for music and recording would keep me away from stores, away from females, and away from cocaine—all three areas of my sickness.

I started to record regular songs first to better understand the recording process and to gain knowledge of the 880. I recorded my first album and called it *Ready or Not*. I named it after my brother's band because I really wanted to impress my brother and his friends in the band. I recorded my music then by creating thirty cassette tapes with the full graphic designs on the tape as well as the J-card insert. I did all the graphic work myself and I was proud of my work because I taught myself through trial and error. I then sold those tapes for ten dollars apiece for a total of $300. I also promised anyone who brought a cassette tape that I would give them a CD. So I had $300 and borrowed another $300 from my sister. I then brought a CD burner. This was a huge purchase back in 1999. The compact disc burners had just come out for consumers to buy, and I was lucky to have one.

I started burning CDs of my music. I had labels or stickers that I applied to the CDs along with creating CD inserts. And

I did all the graphic work! It looked professionally done. I then worked out a deal with the Blockbuster Video in my neighborhood. They shrink-wrapped all my CDs for me. I first gave a CD to those who purchased my cassette tape, as I promised. I then hooked up my family from back at home. They would send me their cassette tapes with their music and I would transfer their recorded data from analog to digital, or in other words I made their cassette tapes into CDs. I told my family about the VS 880 and before I knew it they were having full music studios built in the basements of their homes, all centered around the 880 as their main piece of equipment.

I purchased the 880 to stay out of harm's way and to record my church. I created my own label in Newlight Records and named it after my church. The only problem was the church wasn't seeing my vision. I even recorded others' churches and pastors all while creating a rap group called God's Elite. The group consisted of four members: a minister of music (RIP); an anointed drummer; me, the bass player; and a serious lyricist on the mic. I remember my pastor was delivering his sermon and I could join in as he read scriptures from the Bible. Now, with the church members in attendance, it appeared that I knew the Bible and certain scriptures. They didn't know that I'd just finished recording my guy's usage of these scriptures in my song. In reality, I was just finishing up on the lyrics that were in my song I created!

One of my good friends just happened to be a pastor who read to me Proverbs 3:5-6 and said, "Acknowledge Him in all thy ways and He will direct your path."

I replied, "Okay, break it down for me, Rev," because I didn't understand or comprehend what he said.

He then told me, "Doug, we are all sinners. Regardless of what your sin is, just call on the name of the Lord, even though you're messing up, and He will see you through it."

So all of the time I was getting high I was doing just that. Acknowledging Him in spite of what I was doing. I really wanted to stop using it, I just didn't know how. I had family and friends that told me, "Just stop," but it wasn't that easy.

I recall I was in Dallas, Texas, and I had some free time on my hands. I had driven my 1971 Oldsmobile Cutlass 442 model. This mug was a four-door with a candy paint job, vogue tires, spoke rims, all leather interior, and all original everything. It was clean! I rode around and found some cocaine in the hood, some companionship, and a place where I could smoke. I had to take care of the house first. For those that don't know, I gave a small portion of my cocaine to the owner of the house in exchange for the use of a room or privacy in his home. I was sitting in this room at this table getting high when I could hear this conversation taking place in the other room. Listening hard, I was trying to figure out what they were saying—and what I heard was that they were planning to rob me! They were planning to take my car, take my wallet, and take my jewelry at gunpoint, then lay low for a couple of days.

Now I was either right or I was high tripping. I immediately thought back to hearing my guy trying to holler at my girl, and when I was shot after I heard the assailant coming towards my room before he shot me. I could hear those incidents clearly, so I decided to follow my first instinct. I chose to act on what I thought I was hearing. I gathered up my things and created the element of surprise. I walked into the hallway and as soon as they opened their door I was standing right there with my hand inside my leather coat as if I was gonna pull out a gun and it startled them. I didn't have a damn thing inside my coat. I just acted like I did! That is an old move in Chicago we called that false flaggin!

I told them, "It ain't worth it." I knew that he was hiding his weapon behind his back underneath his shirt. He tried to dismantle the situation but I wasn't moving. He knew that he didn't have enough time to reach behind his back, pull out a gun, take aim and shoot. They didn't know if I actually had a gun; they definitely thought I did. I was determined not to be a victim of another crime, so I proceeded to let myself out of the house and out of that situation. Who knows what would've happened to me had I not heard them plotting in the other room, when they thought they were being discreet? Dallas is always on *The First 48*!

Another incident that occurred was when I borrowed the car, for whatever reason I told my sister. I ended up buying some drugs, but I didn't have enough money. I asked for X amount, which cost X amount of dollars. I was short with the money and I figured I would just drive off fast and everything would be alright. I drove off too fast and the car began to sputter and stall as it coasted down the street. I was trying to start the car as an angry mob was slowly approaching. There were about ten to fifteen guys in my rearview mirror, and one of the guys threw a forty-ounce glass bottle and shattered the rear window completely. About the same time, the car finally started up and I was able to remove myself from that situation. As I returned the keys to my sister, I gave her some lame excuse. I can't even remember what it was and I know she didn't believe me. I didn't care. All I cared about was getting high.

CHAPTER 17

Bad Choices

My addiction or habit was beginning to cost me more money. I had a desire for more drugs. To me, that equals more back and more of me getting my helmet cleaned. So I put together a team of addicts and showed them how they could get high for free and didn't have to put themselves in jeopardy every day. After seeing this happening every day, their confidence levels and hustle were at a high. We started hitting store after store, getting whatever we could. I was feeling like I was standing at the ten-yard line waiting for the kickoff, adrenaline just flowing through me, a feeling that I only felt when I was on the field. This was post-traumatic stress disorder to me!

I didn't know who to turn to or where to go to get help. I was totally lost. I didn't know what to do. As I was getting my team together, I had established a few rules along the way. One rule was the first lick of the day must net at least $170. That money was used to pay for two rooms, buy food, and buy at least fifty dollars' worth of cocaine! Now, fifty dollars of cocaine was a lot in Houston, Texas, at the time. Not everyone was required to go on the lick. Only half the team would go out and the other half would stay behind waiting on the group that left to handle their business.

I had another rule that you must eat your entire breakfast before you could get high. My team used to fuss at me about this rule all the time, but I knew they wouldn't lose much weight if they ate daily. Cocaine suppresses your desire to eat. If you wanted to lose weight in hurry, there was nothing like a crack diet. Appearance is crucial when you go up in these stores. My appearance was crucial to me because I made sure I ate so

I didn't lose any weight. I was able to conceal my addiction behind my looks! I just didn't look like I got high! I had plenty of friends who looked just like me and you could not tell if they got high based on their appearance.

I recall one day that I sent my team on a mission to retrieve dual power window switches from auto parts stores. I then went to purchase a dual power window switch to get a receipt for this item. It cost slightly over $100, which meant they would give you cash back and not a gift card. Once I got the receipt I went to this office-related place called Kinko's and made several copies. I then distributed these receipts to my team with instructions to return the item at different locations throughout the city. I had them return merchandise for the first shift and then the second shift. Second shift was normally a completely different set of employees. This activity went on for several months as I chose different items, repeating the process with each item. I then took my team on the road and we did the exact same thing in the Dallas, Texas, area. We were raking in the money. If you would've seen me, you would've thought I was a drug dealer.

I had big money, and I was happy, and every member of my team was happy. I was also fulfilling all my addiction needs. I had purchased a four-bedroom home. It had a hammock and an orange tree in the backyard. I bought brand new furniture and turned one of my rooms into a music studio. I purchased brand new musical equipment that I rarely used because I was too busy getting high! I was living the good life, yet things began to change. One of my team members was caught and arrested. I was on my way to bond her out when I found out that she was singing like a canary bird. She told them everything that I had done. I was soon arrested and charged with a RICO crime (Racketeering Influenced Corrupt Organizations Act), facing up to twenty years in a Texas prison!

My bond was extremely high and my family didn't really have a clue how much time I was really facing. My family just didn't have the resources or the funds to get me out, so I was forced to use the money I'd accumulated over the years to bond out or pay this lawyer. I decided to pay the lawyer and

I lost everything in the process. I lost my house, my cars, my new furniture, my studio equipment, my suits, my jerseys—everything! I couldn't believe it.

I was locked up in the Harris County Jail, and the time was moving way too slow. I took on a janitor job to make the time go by faster. I needed to do something. Just laying around all day wasn't gonna cut for me. This janitorial job also had the responsibility to serve the food trays to the different pods (areas within the jail where a group of inmates lived). There was this one pod that was noticeably different from the other pods. It held members of the Mexican Mafia and MS-13. They were wearing shades and hats and Air Jordans in jail. That was unheard of!

I was performing my duties one day when the leader made a gesture for me to come to him. He then told me that there was a shipment of tobacco coming through and he needed me to pick it up and drop it off. He told me that I would be taken care of. Tobacco was a very popular item inside the jail. If you had tobacco or other drugs you had power, so I agreed to transfer the tobacco. The leader also asked me for my inmate identification number and all my information. I didn't want any problems, but I'll admit I was a little scared. Later on that day, I picked up and dropped off three huge bags of pipe tobacco. I knew it was pipe tobacco because one of my uncles used to always smoke it in his pipe.

After I performed this task, time went by and I ended up paying my lawyer a huge sum of money and the RICO charges were dropped to a robbery. I went from a possible twenty-year sentence to a possible five-year sentence. That's the deal my lawyer got for me, only I had to plead guilty and face time being locked up. It was up to the judge. Five years was still a long time. I entered a guilty plea and was shipped off to the Texas Department of Corrections (TDC) Garza West Unit to serve a two-year sentence. I was still an addict trying to deal with my addiction. I knew this sentence would give me time to reflect upon the choices I made that landed me in the penitentiary.

In the meantime, $300 was added to my books or account by the Mexican Mafia. This money was added because of what

I had done for them in transferring that tobacco. My inmate number was 01413712. I had fallen from the top to the bottom. I was shoulder to shoulder with murderers, child molesters, gang bangers, rapists, robbers, and drug dealers. I just couldn't believe it. Even though a few family members knew and were embarrassed by the whole incident, they covered for me.

I was really uncomfortable with lying in bed all day just watching television, so I got a job within the system to help my time go by a little faster. I had accepted a position in the laundry room, but right away I noticed there was too much helmet cleaning going on in there. The gay inmates were having a ball, so I immediately quit that job. Then the maintenance coordinator had found out somehow that I had a degree and he selected me to be his new clerk. This was a prestigious position within the system so I took it. I had access to everything you can think of—way more than the average inmate.

I worked that job for several months like a regular job until I got into it with one of the inmates and spent thirty days in the hole. That's solitary confinement, a small cell where you are all alone by yourself, so I started writing music, songs like "My Life, My Decision," "Teardrops," "Send You Me," "He Will Provide," and "Hurt So Bad," to name a few. I started crying immediately after I wrote "You Are Loved" because I knew that it wasn't me that wrote that song. It was the God in me! All of these songs and a host of other songs I wrote can be heard at www.reverbnation.com/dsmooove. When you have time, check out some of my music.

CHAPTER 18
Chaplain's Assistant

My thirty days were up. I had finally gotten out of the hole and back with the general population. In the hole you don't have anything but your mat that you slept on, a blanket, toilet paper, and pencil and paper. I was finally free from that situation. I was back to banging beats on the table and writing songs. Some of the inmates were impressed and listened to the songs that I had written, while there were others who simply didn't care. I was just glad to be out of solitary confinement. When you're all by yourself, all you can do is think, and I was thinking about everything.

The chaplain must've been looking through the inmate records and found that I'd graduated from college. I was chosen to be the chaplain's assistant and I know that I didn't apply for the position. So now that I was his assistant, it meant I would be doing some work for the Lord in prison! I was responsible for some paperwork that involved the distribution of Bibles and setting up his equipment for church services every Sunday. I was also in charge and able to listen to music that was being played at the church services on Sundays. I added some new songs that were different at the time. I remember "Stomp" by Kirk Franklin was one. It was one of the more popular songs, and I played it every Sunday. There was also another song that I found and played every Sunday. This song was also very popular amongst the inmates. It was called "I Can Only Imagine" by Mercy Me.

I became immersed in my duties and time actually flew by. God was working with me and I didn't know it. I was released after eleven months in that place. I can remember getting out and the first song I heard was played to me by my family. I will never forget It. The song was titled "We Fall Down" by Donnie McClurkin. I was able to listen to this song and the lyrics were really motivational to me. The message was very clear: We fall down, but we get up! I had fallen down as low as I could possibly go, and now it was time for me to get back up.

When I was released after eleven months, I had to stay in a halfway house. For months I had to follow their rules and their ways. I hated it! I was committed to their twelve-step program. Yet it was difficult for me. I started off as a client but ended up as the director of administration. Yeah, they hired me to work for them. It was right up my alley. I was a functional addict. I ended up working there for a few months. I eventually ended up raising three boys whose fathers were noticeably absent in their lives. My lawyer had advised me to get out of Texas, if I could, to avoid serving longer sentences for petty crimes in the future. I was very hesitant at first; I just didn't want to leave my only child. I knew her mom would take good care of her. I just knew I needed to move on in order for me to stay out of the Texas system. I knew they were just waiting for me as I watched a few of my friends get caught up and receive X amount of time. More time than what they should have served, that's for sure. It was only a matter of time until they got to me too, and I didn't want to be considered guilty by association.

I thought about my family of musicians and the guys that I knew back at home in Waukegan, Illinois, that played music. It weighed on me every day what was I gonna do, so I made a tough decision to move back home to Illinois. I didn't know what I was gonna do for employment, but I was known throughout the community and wanted to make a difference. A relative of mine somehow knew about my struggles, so he hooked me up with some back and I had my helmet cleaned at his apartment. The next morning he had to go to the city and he needed me to ride with him, so we went to Chicago and this mug ended up at Soldier Field, the home of the Chicago Bears. He must've found out that I hadn't watched an NFL game in over a decade. It was hard for me to watch a game knowing that I was right there and should've been participating.

Here I was at Soldier Field. I had no clue who the Bears were playing, I just knew that it was cold. Then I realized that we didn't have regular seats. We were down on the field and in the tunnel as if I were playing. This was major to my psyche in getting over the fact that I could've been playing in the NFL. I was able to watch a game from a player's perspective as we watched from the sidelines. It did help that it was against the Dallas Cowboys, my childhood favorite team, and it was a playoff game. The Cowboys won the game. But being there on the sidelines did wonders for me psychologically.

I recall I was home looking for a job when I came across a teaching job at the Youth Conservation Corps (YCC). I knew that it was going to be difficult for me to get that job now that I had a felony conviction on my record, but I applied for the job anyway. I was interviewed and I got the position in spite of having a felony in my background. I was shocked that I was able to work with kids again, educating them on life skills and different job opportunities. God was showing me favor back then, but I just didn't know it. I was thinking now that I had a record, my teaching career was over.

My first year of teaching in my hometown I was able to assist twenty males in obtaining employment. I was also able to educate over 2,300 younger elementary kids and teach them first aid and safety. For my efforts I was nominated for the Tom Joyner Hardest Worker Award, an award that the nationally syndicated radio personality gave out once a month. One of my students nominated me. Somehow, I won this award! I was really shocked and surprised. I was selected out of over hundreds of thousands applicants. I received a check for $1,000, as well as a plaque, and I was interviewed by Tom Joyner. The interview was featured on his website. This honor was huge to me. I was back at home doing positive things within my community, and nobody knew all the things I had gone through. This interview can also be heard at www.reverbnation.com/dsmooove.

I was doing positive things within my community, but I was also still getting high and getting my helmet cleaned and stuff. Every time I went to the store I would buy something and I would steal something too, even though I had the money to pay for it! That hadn't changed. There were also many of my friends that I took with me and got their helmet cleaned or some back, whichever they preferred. This was free of charge. I could very easily name twenty to twenty-five guys that went along with me over the years—you know who you are! I was addicted to the lifestyle. They all got their helmets cleaned just because they were hanging out with me or had some form of cocaine. I didn't discriminate either. I had all different races of women that I could choose from. It was crazy! I even had different women call me to come over, get high, and clean my helmet for me. Real talk. These ladies were functional addicts with jobs and careers. I wasn't dealing with no hood rats. These were reputable women in the community. You would be surprised if I revealed their names!

There were times I would spend money and times I wouldn't take a dime out of my pocket. I recall I had a close friend whom I would pick up and take with me to get high, get some back, and get his helmet cleaned. He was a teammate of mine and one of the first people that I got high with. At the time he was stressed, depressed, and just really down on his luck. I also helped him get a couple jobs while I was back at home. He knew a lot about me and I knew a lot about him. I remember I got off work early and stopped by his house to get high. As I approached his crib I could hear him talking on the speaker phone to what sounded like my lady friend. It was a complete violation of our friendship and we were not raised that way! To me it was *déjà vu* all over again. Was I high tripping, or did I hear my guy talking to my girl? I confronted them both and they both denied my accusation. They told me that I was high tripping!

As time moved on I would eventually catch those two together after she lied to me on a phone call earlier that same day. I was really shocked as to what I had found. All I could do was deal with it the best way that I could and move on. I went and got high, then I went and talked to my dad. Did I tell you that I tried the twelve-step program two times and failed each time? I was gonna try the program for a third time when a friend of mine told me that was the definition of insanity! According to Albert Einstein, insanity is doing the same thing over and over while expecting different results.

I was getting ready to go back and try a twelve-step rehabilitation program in the Lake County Health Department building. I'd tried the program before, but my friend had made a good point to me, so I ended up just getting away from the area for an extended period of time. I was gonna stay at her house and have everyone that really knew me thinking I was in rehabilitation getting help for my addictions. Little did I know she was on a mission. She knew that I really liked getting my helmet cleaned and this is what she liked to do. We must've stopped at a road stop about three of four times on our way to her house. I was indulging every day. I remember we had this conversation and she asked me what was the most amount of times that I had ejaculated in one calendar day. I had to think back to my college days when it happened seven times! She was then on a mission the next day to break that personal record of mine.

I'll spare you all the details and stuff; however, I will say that she would put this cream in her throat, tie her hair up, and clean my helmet for me. We did this process over and over all day and all night long. I couldn't believe it. When the day was finally over and we tallied up ten times! That's right, ten times, as in Harring-ten. I just couldn't believe it. I had met my match. I was thinking it was too bad that she stayed out of town very far away from me.

73

CHAPTER 19
Opposite of Hott Production

I was looking for a job. My time teaching was up. I knew that the contract I signed was about to expire, so I started plotting and scheming on ways I could hit a lick! I was looking to be hired by Goodwill. I needed to make more money than what I was making as a teacher at YCC. I was contacted by the state representative who happened to work for Goodwill too at the time. She interviewed me for a legislative assistant position that was available. She told me that the position required office work, computer work, and a great deal of work within the community. This was an opportunity for me to give back and assist many people. I got the job and right off the bat she had me working within the community. God was showing me favor then but I just didn't know it.

One of the things I really liked was her dress code. I had to wear a shirt and tie. This was right up my alley. I stayed clean! I was a functional addict functioning at the highest level. I had guys coming to me complaining about their criminal record. Well, I had an album, explaining my background as well. I knew that I would also need music to keep me busy and out of harm's way, so I started recording daily. I knew that if I was making music then I wasn't getting high or trying to get my helmet cleaned.

I started playing the bass guitar at the church. This church was bigger than the two churches combined that I used to play for in Houston. I was going to choir rehearsal at Jesus Name Apostolic Church in Waukegan, Illinois. As I was going to rehearsal, somebody was going into my apartment that I was sharing with my lady and doing whatever. I couldn't really prove it, but I'm not stupid. I saw too many signs. In the meantime, my uncle was retiring from the family band. They wanted my brother to step in so they could continue to play. Unfortunately, my brother was not feeling it at the time. He was too busy trying to get his company Opposite of Hott Production off the ground. What's the opposite of hott? Cold, right?

Well, we were as cold as the name, and my brother accumulated an enormous amount of talent. We had two full-fledged recording studios that we operated: Studio A and Studio B. Studio A was the larger of the two, and we would utilize this studio for our larger groups. It had a soundproof booth complete with a variety of guitars and top-of-the-line keyboards, drum machines, and equipment. Studio B was also called the igloo. It was a smaller studio, complete with a soundproof booth known as the cooler and a variety of bass guitars, top-of-the-line keyboards, drum machines, and equipment. We had a feature website with two locations to record. We recorded albums, videos, mixtapes, commercials—everything! We had different producers creating music. We were doing photo shoots too.

We were making money using the God-given talent we all had. This went on for years. I was happy yet I was still fighting my demons. I created a group called the Harrington Connection. It consisted of me, my brother, and my two nephews—our version of my uncles' the Thomas Brothers Band.

We recorded a CD and I took a cassette tape of my uncles' and ran it through the computer and made their music into a CD. This was huge because my uncles never really recorded their music. They never recorded a CD. I put their faces on one CD and our faces on another cold CD. We ended up creating double CDs and passing them out to family members for Christmas. This music can also be heard at www.reverbnation.com/harringtonconnection.

In the meantime, my uncle was retiring from the family band and they wanted my brother to replace him. My brother told me that I should take the spot and show them what I learned over the years. He knew that I could get down. They didn't know that I could play on their level. To me, this was an opportunity to fulfill a childhood dream. I always wanted to play with my uncles. They had a show coming up in Chicago and I had one rehearsal in which to get ready. I didn't know any of the songs, but I could play every song that they rehearsed. I knew I had the skills and the ability to play back whatever I heard. It was a gift that I had from God, and I wowed them. They didn't know that their nephew was that good! I knew that I could play with the big dogs. I had the skills and the confidence to perform on stage from playing in front of the church each Sunday. I had the respect and support of my dad and my brother and now I had my uncles' approval too, something I'd always wanted.

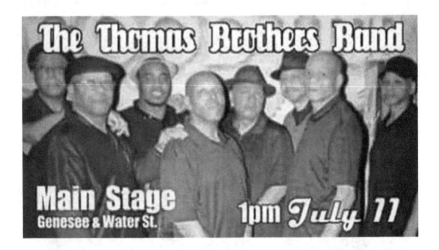

The Thomas Brothers Band was known throughout the Chicagoland and the Cook County area. I had a vision of them being known throughout Lake County, where I lived, too, and I was on a mission to make that happen. I remember that I used to watch different bands perform, only to say that my uncles' band sounded just as good if not better than the band I was watching. I was now the bass player and a part of that band.

It was a challenge to me to get the band heard. I enlisted the help of a friend who also managed bands and with his assistance we played all over the county. The Thomas Brothers Band was jamming wherever we played. I really enjoyed playing with my uncles. I had some of the best times in my life just hanging out with them. We played all over the county.

The losses in my life began at this time. First, we lost one of my uncles who was a prominent band member. His loss was devastating to the entire family and the band. Then I lost a real close friend of mine. I remember we both were at the Universal Soul Circus on a Friday doing the family thing. He was with his family and I was with my girl and her grandkids. We were gonna hook up again on Monday, but I got to the office that Monday morning and a close friend called me and told me that my friend had died. I couldn't believe it. I was just with him. He was a true friend, one that I could depend on, and a teammate. I then lost a brother-in-law and was unable to attend his funeral. Then I lost my best friend and my rock, my dad. I was experiencing all of these losses back-to-back.

The death of my father was really tough for me because now I had no one to talk to about my problems. I recall my father was sick and in the hospital and he had me sneaking him food. Pops was crazy! He had a spirit about him that just made you love him. He had this personality and charisma that was crazy yet beautiful. One day he asked me where my brother was and why he didn't come to see him. He and my brother weren't speaking to each other at the time my dad became sick. For decades my brother would stop over to my dad's apartment when he got off work to drink a beer with him. I explained to Pops that my brother was in the intensive care unit of the same hospital he was in. He then tried to convince the nurse to take him to the ICU area to see his oldest son. It almost worked, as he charmed the female nurse on duty into taking him down there. He couldn't, however, charm her male supervisor.

My dad eventually passed away and it was really tough for my family! We had to postpone my dad's funeral a few days until my brother was strong enough to attend. I remember that I had already booked the band to perform on the big stage at North Chicago Community Days, and my dad's funeral was the same day! It was crazy emotional for me. It was one of the most difficult things that I ever had to do in my life. I had to lay my dad to rest, then I had to perform with my uncles.

CHAPTER 20
An Addict

An addict is often portrayed as a skinny, dirty, nappy-headed, begging bum from the streets. This is far from the truth. Most of the addicts I knew were just the opposite. They had nice builds, clean-cut hair, and worked in nine-to-five professional environments. They looked just like you! You would be surprised if you knew all the people who were functional drug addicts. I'm not the one who thinks that I'm better than the next addict. I know there are plenty of people that used to do this or that and now lead a sober life. I will be one of those people! An addiction is a disease that should be treated as a disease.

Cocaine wasn't the only drug available. The defense, diesel, or a shirt were all different names to describe the drug heroin, which was also available. I knew heroin users as well. There were just as many users of this drug who were holding it down and still using it. Heroin was just their drug of choice. I wasn't one who acted differently towards heroin users. I tried it once and it made me sick. I didn't like the high. I recall a good friend of mine overdosed on heroin and almost died, only to be saved by a shot of Narcan. He is clean now, and to see him have another chance at life is very encouraging.

I remember I was at Gurnee Mills shopping mall when this lady called out my entire name. "Doug Harrington!" she said with excitement in her voice. She was excited to see me as I tried to remember her name and where I'd known her from. She took me back to Glen Flora Elementary School and said there was a group of black girls who wanted to beat her up. I stood up for her and would not allow it to happen. She said that I even walked her home after school to ensure her safety for a couple of days. She wanted to thank me for my actions way back then. She told me I was her guardian angel and she was now a pastor's wife. Praise God!

In the meantime, my brother mentioned to me that he had some Mint Condition (a rhythm and blues band from Minneapolis) tickets for his wife and himself, but he wanted me to have them because he thought that he would still be in the hospital when the concert date came around, so he gave me the tickets. I noticed that the date of the concert was months away, so I challenged him to get well so we could attend the concert together. He worked his tail off and got out the week of the concert. My family didn't think he should go out in public so soon but we were determined to go. Mint Condition was his favorite band. I decided that I was gonna try and do something special for my big brother. I wrote a letter to Mint Condition's management informing them how my brother had fought and regained his health using the concert as his motivation. I finished the letter, left my contact number, and went to work. Once I was at work I realized that I had forgotten my cell phone at home. I had completed my duties as an assistant to the state representative and returned home. As I picked up my phone I had seven messages, all from Mint Condition's management. They wanted to meet my brother backstage after the concert! We were issued backstage passes and a host of other perks. It was very gratifying to sit back and watch him meet his favorite band. We were backstage for a while and I took pictures of my brother with the band.

My brother died a few months later and I was devastated. I was in his hospital room holding his hand when he died. As the nurse announced he was gone, my mother grabbed me and hugged me like never before. I then went home. I remember I was getting high and I didn't want to live. I had turned off every light in my apartment. It was pitch black. Have you seen the movie *Ghost* with Whoopi Goldberg, Patrick Swayze, and Demi Moore? Well, there is a scene in this movie where this guy is surrounded by evil, dark images of the Grim Reaper. Well, I was sitting in the dark in this chair just crying away. I had stood up to cut the lights on when I saw these black images surrounding me, just like in the movie. Then there was this white light that looked like a ribbon and some smoke. It maneuvered its way in between the dark figures and around me. I didn't understand because there was no light on, yet I could see this bright light shining. It was crazy! The dark figures had disappeared and I cut on the light. I immediately sat down and thought to myself, *Was I just high tripping, or did I see what I thought I saw?*

I recall another situation where I knew I was being watched but I couldn't identify the equipment watching me. So I took something that did not belong to me in my efforts to continue getting high. I knew that I was being recorded, hoping that something would be done to help me. Nothing was done; however, something was said. In fact, there was a post about the incident and I responded by saying "a damn fool," and I knew who it was referring to. I don't think it was known that I knew. I also missed a family reunion in Detroit, Michigan, that I wanted to attend because my addictions wouldn't let me attend.

I recall that I'd just finished cutting the grass one day and I was talking with a family member afterward. I was told that I was the strongest person that he knew. I don't how we got on that topic, but a few weeks later my daughter told me the exact same thing! She even went into details explaining to me why I was the strongest man she'd ever known. This meant a lot to me with her knowing my addictions and shortcomings.

There was also an incident where a really close friend was trying to holler at my lady at times when I was away. I addressed the individual involved and he apologized for his actions. About three weeks later, he was at it again. I addressed him again, but I was really hurt by his actions. I didn't have anyone that I could talk to about it. I couldn't believe it; he was very close to me and my family. I was smart enough to charge it to the game, knowing that he was suffering from the same addiction that I was suffering from.

CHAPTER 21
Stroke Victim

It was June 11, 2019, and I wasn't feeling very well. I turned myself in to the hospital for evaluation. I called my daughter to let her know I was at the hospital and I was having some tests done. I assumed everything was going to be alright. I told them that I was having chest pains and breathing problems, knowing that they had to keep me overnight as a patient if I said this. I stayed overnight as planned. Later that day, I was discharged from the hospital. I was headed home when I got a phone call from a friend. She wanted me to come over, get high, and clean my helmet. "I'm really not feeling well," I explained, as I was just leaving the hospital. But me being me, I wasn't about turn down a free high, and she was good too! So I pulled up on her as she requested, then she changed gears on me. When I arrived, she cooked me dinner. I was shocked because she had never cooked for me before. I ate the meal and became real sleepy. I ended up falling asleep on the couch watching ESPN. I didn't even get my helmet cleaned that night.

I woke up the next morning and went to the crib. I recall arriving at home and calling up my guy to put in my order. I had done this so many times before. He brought over my goods and I proceeded to get high. I still wasn't feeling well and I was also hungry, so I gathered some snacks and headed back into my room to eat and to watch some ESPN highlights. About twenty minutes later I began to feel really funny. My breathing and my legs were feeling funny as I cried out to my mom to call 911. I fell to the ground and I lost consciousness. I was out for days! I was on a ventilator, unable to breathe for myself and totally paralyzed. I was told that several people came into my room and prayed for me.

I was having a serious dream when I was out. At first, I was looking for my brother and my dad. I heard them but I couldn't find them. The dream was wild! I was asleep and not aware of what was happening, so I contacted my daughter to get her perspective on things that occurred and this is what she said:

"On June eleventh, I got a message from you. You were in the hospital because of your heart. Turns out, you had a mini stroke. We did a video call and you were still in the hospital getting ready to be discharged soon, and it seemed like you were doing okay at that moment. I spoke with your sister shortly after that and we booked a flight for me and my son to come visit and spend a little time with you. Your situation scared me, honestly! We had plans to leave Houston, Texas, and come to Waukegan, Illinois, that Saturday to visit. It was supposed to be a surprise! And to my surprise, my world literally came crashing down. You suffered a massive stroke and things weren't looking good. I remember our flight finally making it to Chicago and we finally made it to the hospital. I walked into your room and saw you with all these tubes and cords attached and I got teary-eyed just seeing you like that! Grandma tried to wake you up, but you wouldn't wake up, so she said, 'There's someone here to see you.'

"You still wouldn't wake up until I said, 'Hey Daddy,' and when you heard my voice you opened your eyes, praise God. The blood pressure machine started making noise. I took it as if you were excited I was there. The doctors came into your room to explain to me your situation. The doctor basically said in so many words to prepare for your funeral. They said that you would be in a paralyzed state for the rest of your life, in and out of different nursing homes until you died. My heart was literally broken and I took it real hard. The doctors left your room when I heard Grandma say to my aunt that she didn't want you to suffer. I left and went outside to call my mom, crying so hard I couldn't even speak. We stayed around the family for a while, praying you would get better. When I left to go back home, I honestly thought that was going to be the last time I saw you alive."

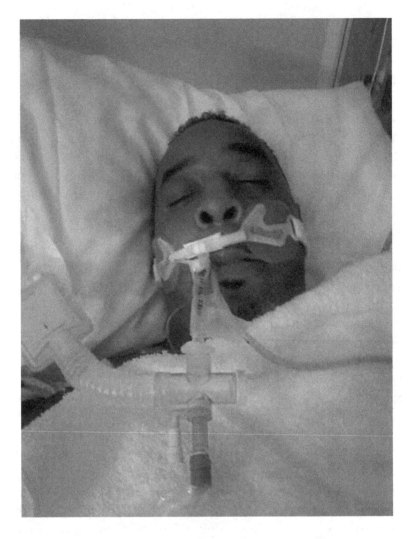

Laying in that bed was tough. I remember that I couldn't move. I heard the doctor telling my family that they were gonna give me an MRI to see if I had any brain activity before they pulled the plug on me. I then heard my daughter and my grandson say goodbye to me like I never heard it before. I wanted to respond and tell them that I was gonna be alright, but I couldn't move at all. I couldn't even open my eyes. I just heard her crying and I was mad because I couldn't hold her, console her, and tell her that I was gonna be okay.

A few minutes had passed and I could tell that my bed was moving. I knew I was heading to get that MRI done. I had to show some form of brain activity. I thought the best way for me to do this was to think of any and everything I could think of. I was thinking of all kinds of stuff as I was hoping to show brain activity. I knew that I had a praying mother and two praying sisters on my side! The movement had stopped and I could tell that I was inside this machine. I was thinking and thinking, hoping that I was showing the brain activity that I needed to show.

When my eyes finally opened, I can remember I was going down this hallway into this ambulance. When they got me situated, I couldn't move any of my body. I was talking and communicating with the doctors through my eyes, one blink for no and two blinks for yes. I was 98% paralyzed! I couldn't move anything. Later on my mom explained to me what happened to me. I was blessed to be alive. I had a little movement in my left foot and my left hand. My sisters started telling me to keep on moving my foot and my hand. I was constantly moving both. This went on for months. I couldn't comprehend how I was able to bench press over 300 pounds one day to struggling to lift three pounds the next. I just couldn't understand it. I wasn't strong enough to even press the television remote to change the channel! It felt crazy to me.

My sisters created some phrase cards for me so that I could better communicate with my family and the staff. These cards were filled with simple commands because I couldn't talk for some reason. Come to find out they cut a hole in my throat so I could breathe. I continued to move my body, attempting to get physically stronger. That's when I really realized that the entire right side of my body wouldn't move for me. Then it hit me that I couldn't walk. I was still unable to comprehend how a man who could rap now couldn't talk! And how I used to run eighty-yard touchdowns but now I couldn't walk! I had a hard time understanding that. My sisters then started to recite each letter of the alphabet in an attempt for me to hold a conversation with them and spell out my needs. This went on for a few days.

I did try writing and it was a joke! I couldn't even write my own name. Then my mom drew up this letter board in which I would spell out my needs. I would simply point at each letter and spell out what I was trying to say.

CHAPTER 22

How I Met God

I went from a letter board to a tablet with a speaking app. Remember, I couldn't talk right now but I can do all things through Christ! The tablet was too large for me to handle with just one hand. I only had one hand, y'all; remember, my entire right side was paralyzed. I installed the same speaking app that was on my tablet into my cell phone. I was finally able to comfortably communicate to my family and the staff who was taking care of me. It was huge for me because now I got to say exactly what I meant and be understood. I didn't have to play charades anymore or take others back to high school class just to have a conversation or answer a question.

The downside to texting the staff was I had only one hand so texting my message to whomever took time. It took longer than it would normally take for a simple message. It didn't really matter to me; I was glad to finally be heard. I had a few family members and close friends and musicians stop by to see me. It was really tough for me to see any of them. My family restricted my visitors, so it was impossible to see me if my family didn't know you. This was actually kinda good for me. It prevented certain people from seeing me.

I had a CNA who was the daughter of one of my guys I grew up with. She explained to her coworkers that I was a friend of her dad, so they took real good care of me. In fact, they actually spoiled me. I hated to leave them, but it was time. I was moved to another facility that supplied me with a motorized wheelchair, y'all. Months went by, then they moved this guy in my room. I had several roommates before, but he was different. He was praying in the presence of his mom, yet he was still using and thought I didn't know! This guy was cool at times but I knew better. He spent more time in the bathroom than he did in our actual room. At times I would hear him call and place his order, and for a couple of days he would go in and out of the bathroom getting high. He didn't think I knew what he was doing because I couldn't walk or talk. He thought that I was scared and intimidated, like he intimidated the staff. Y'all just don't know how bad I wanted to check him and show him, but I just was physically unable to. Plus, I was trying to be a bigger, better person. He would spend the next few days in bed recuperating from his antics. I saw myself in his behavior. I wasn't about to tell or snitch on him because he was no different than I was.

Sometimes we tend to take for granted the little things in life. Having a stroke has been nothing but craziness for me. I had to start everything all over again. It's like I'm trapped inside a child's body. I had to learn how to swallow, eat, and drink all over again. They were feeding me through a tube connected to my stomach. Then I was eating "para food," as they called it; I called it baby food.

My thinking, or my mind, now is better than ever. It's been clean, free from any outside pollutants or mind-altering chemicals known as drugs, for about three years now. I have therapy every day in the mornings except the weekend. I'm working out with my physical therapist. I'm currently wearing a diaper—a damn diaper, y'all! I'm raised in the air like I'm some cattle and placed into my wheelchair. Did I mention they gave me a motorized wheelchair too? Top of the line. To me it's a motor scooter! I be scooting around all over the place. I still haven't figured out how to pop a wheelie yet, but I'm trying... It has been crazy for me.

Imagine you can't walk. You can't go anywhere you want to go. You can't go upstairs. You can't go down stairs. It's crazy, man! I can't even turn over in my bed right now, because my right side is still paralyzed. I can't talk either! Just imagine someone took away your ability to talk and communicate. You're trying to convince anyone and in your mind you're saying it, using gestures and stuff, and you feel like you're playing a game of charades! It's very frustrating. I use my text-to-speak app and basically it conveys what I'm typing into my cell phone into words or verbal communication. My cell phone is talking for me. It's been crazy, man, and most of the time the person you're talking to doesn't have the time to stand there and wait for you to type out whatever it is that you're trying to say. Or they may have already said something that you want to respond to, but you haven't finished with the first response and they ask you or say something else. It's crazy, man!

I believe I've had more disagreements and arguments with my family in the past month than I have in my entire fifty-four years on this earth! It's also very frustrating because you know they have your back and best interest at heart. It's hard for me to believe but this is what my life has been like the past few years. That's far from playing my bass guitar or going to the studio. I remember getting high every day, getting me some back, or my helmet cleaned daily! It was like I had an on-demand remote for sex! Whenever, whatever, wherever I wanted it, I had it. All I had to do was ask, make a call, or pull the truck over somewhere. This behavior went on for years, so me being without was definitely needed in order for me to deal with my sexual addiction.

All the women that I had in my sexual lifestyle have been removed. I realize that I no longer have the desire to have sex or to get high anymore. I had been praying for years for God to remove my desire to get high! He may not come when you want Him but He is always on time. I no longer was plotting the desire to get my helmet cleaned or get me some back. That desire was gone! I no longer had the temptation or thoughts I once had. I am finally clean for the first time in about forty-five years, and it feels so good to me. Even when I was locked up for eleven months, I was still getting high. No more getting high to stimulate and increase the sexual experience.

I knew it was gonna take an act of God to remove me from my addictions. I tried everything. However, I did have an idea of how it would happen to me—I'm talking about the stroke. I just didn't exactly know how or when it was going to happen. Before the stroke, I was in the kitchen with my nephew. We were both hooking up something to eat, and I just went blank and hit the kitchen floor. Bam! I was out. I quickly came to and hopped back on my feet. My nephew asked me, "Are you okay?" It was scary yet crazy. I really didn't know what to do.

I just recently visited a good friend of mine who'd suffered a stroke. He was in good spirits and everything. Now it has happened to me! I'm grateful that it has finally happened to me. And Lord, I thank you. Things have finally changed in my life, and Lord, I thank you! You see there is a wheelchair right here and I'm in that wheelchair! I can't walk on my own or use the bathroom by myself, yet I say, "Lord, I thank you!" I know some folks may say this or that, but they don't know what all I've been through and I'm still alive. That's why I say thank you! It could have been easy for me to praise Him when I was up and on my feet and in the end zone. I scored thirty-six touchdowns in my college career. I was inducted along with my teammates into the Midland University Hall of Fame.

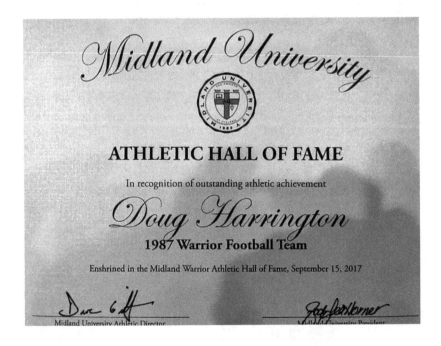

Midland University

ATHLETIC HALL OF FAME

In recognition of outstanding athletic achievement

Doug Harrington

1987 Warrior Football Team

Enshrined in the Midland Warrior Athletic Hall of Fame, September 15, 2017

Midland University Athletic Director

Midland University President

Now I can't walk and I can't talk, yet I say thank you, Lord! I have another chance to live life. Those who know me know that I will tell you upfront. That's just the type of man I am. Once I set my mind on something, it will be accomplished. I had my mind set years ago, but my body and flesh weren't on the same page and out of control. It prevented me all these years. Y'all remember when I referred to the movie *Ghost*, I was surrounded by evil, and I saw this white ribbon of light in total darkness. That was confirmation for me that it was bigger than me.

As time moved on, I started feeling sorry for myself. "Boo-hoo, why did this happen to me!" I started crying out. I thought I was missing out on something. I realized that the people I thought were gonna be there for me were not there at all. It was a smack in the face and a wakeup call that I needed. First, I lost two of my cousins. Then one of my close friends was murdered. Then I lost two more close friends that I grew up with. Then I lost a high school teammate that I played football with. I also lost one of my favorite uncles. I couldn't attend either one's funeral because I just had a massive stroke, was bedridden, and COVID-19 hit the country. I had people praying for me as my family and friends were dying around me. I went from feeling sorry about myself and the situation to motivated to do better.

A friend of mine told me that God saved you for a reason. He only uses His strongest soldiers to fight His toughest battles. Who else can say that they dealt with the indiscretion of a close friend on several occasions, and survived two stab wounds, five gunshot wounds, incarceration, a massive stroke, and lived to talk about it? I had the opportunity to play in the National Football League only to go to the penitentiary, and God was with me every step along the way. I went from running eighty yards to the end zone to my wheelchair. He was waiting for me to acknowledge Him and establish a personal relationship with Him. The reason why I'm going through it is because I'm on my way to it! I was 98% paralyzed—98%! I couldn't move, I couldn't do anything. I was talking to my doctor by blinking my eyes.

I'm slowly regaining the use of my right side of my body. For two years it wouldn't move at all or have any feeling within it. Now it's moving and I have feeling in it. Praise God. I'm currently only about 42% paralyzed. I know I have a great deal of work to do, and I'm focused on doing it. I just wanna walk again, talk again, and play my bass guitar again. Remember, my daughter was told to prepare for my funeral, but God had other plans for me.

I'm not gonna act like I'm all holy and what not, act like I'm better than the next man, or I'm gonna live a long time. I was supposed to be gone a long time ago. But God's mercy kept me here from harm's way. I was texting a good friend of mine right after I was FaceTiming my tears to another close friend of forty-five or so years. He said, "Smooth, only the strong survive and you are one of those survivors. Your demons, you faced them head on and won that battle, Smooove. We all have our sins and flaws, bro, but we were raised different, cut from a different cloth! We all have skeletons in our closet, so you aren't alone, bro. We have over forty-five strong years of friendship and counting. You were the one who taught me how to tote that football. This book is going to touch a lot of people's souls, man. I'm proud of you, bro. Ya digg!"

Now I feel blessed to be a part of the birth and growth of my granddaughter, to be able to watch her and her brother. It's all the motivation that I need to succeed. I look forward to my weekend FaceTime calls from my daughter so that I can see my grandkids. I can't talk so it means everything to me. Just recently my grandson hit his first game-winning free throws the other day, and I was so proud of him and happy. He needs to know that's how it all started. A good friend of mine saw this (I had posted the video of his game on my Facebook page). He said, "It runs in your family!" One of my old coaches said that he was just following in my footsteps. Hopefully, this book will help him not to make the same mistakes I made!

I realize that God saved me on numerous occasions. I have come a long way in my recovery from this stroke. I have an even longer way to go. I know that there will be some rough days ahead of me, but I'm ready to take on that challenge. He has something for me.

I would like to thank all of you for taking your time and reading my story. I left out some things that should have been said, but I just plain forgot. I'm blessed that I can text and have a conversation with my daughter and my son. I will one day talk verbally to them again. This whole situation has made me an even stronger man. I believe that one day I will walk and talk again! I ask that you keep me in your prayers. God never changes. God is too real to ignore. I am a believer in God!

And if you don't know, now you know.
God is good all the time, and all the time God is good!

CHAPTER 23

Front cover design created by Gary McKelvey.

SPECIAL THANKS TO

Joyce Edmonds
DaQuoiya Harrington
Donna Harrington
Damon Harrington
Shevela Hunter
Melissa Thompson
Gary McKelvey
Terry Wright
Jimmy Sawyers
Michael Martin
Kenny Curry
Melvin Buck Yancey
Greg Vickers
Barry Beckwith
Ira Williams
Edwin Wilson
Edgar Hobbs
Kenny Hamilton
Darren Gibson
Derrick Moore
Michael Springs
Dwayne Springs
Don Cullen Thompson
Walter Goldstein
Byron Crump
Mike Paulsen
Andy White
Donnie Paulsen
Michael Blackmon
Curtis Cooper
Ralph McLean
Anthony Wright

Clarence "Grasshoppa" Williams
Esko Shepard
Marcus Kemp
Darryl Adams
Bernard "Buddy" Carpenter
Rita "Bosslady" Mayfield
Cara Churchich-Riggs
Shelby Riggs
Brittany Adams, Jamie Clark, and Nicole Jurasik at Warren Barr
My physical therapists, Elizabeth Duran and Raymond Santos
Lourdes Ruiz
Tiffany Robinson
Reena John
Nurse Joy
Joe
Jomund
Meghan
David Wigs
Gustavo Moran
Daniel Roman
Pedro Tony Roman
the staff at the Landmark of Des Plains
and to anyone else I may have forgotten
please charge it to my head and not my heart

My music and Tom Joyner interview can be heard at
www.reverbnation.com/dsmooove or www.reverbnation.com/
harringtonconnection.

Review Requested:
We'd like to know if you enjoyed the book. Please consider leaving a review on the platform from which you purchased the book.